was an archaeological and architectural project of
monumental proportions—and a project in which
the quest for accuracy was often considered less
appealing than the quest for beauty.

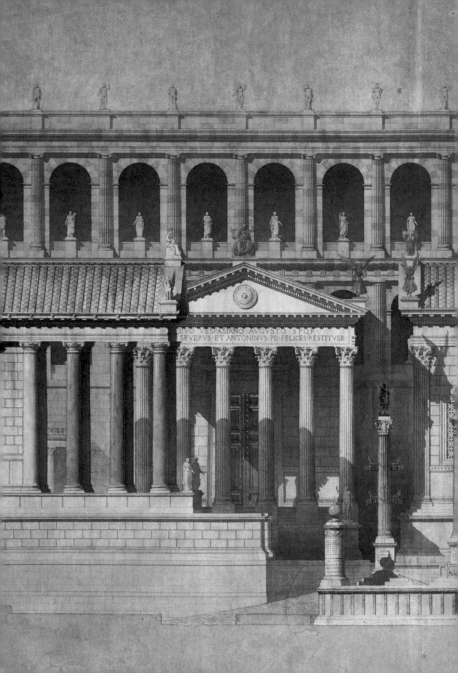

DIVO · VESPASIANO · AVGVSTO · SPQR ·
SEVERVS · ET · ANTONINVS · PII · FELICES · RESTITVER

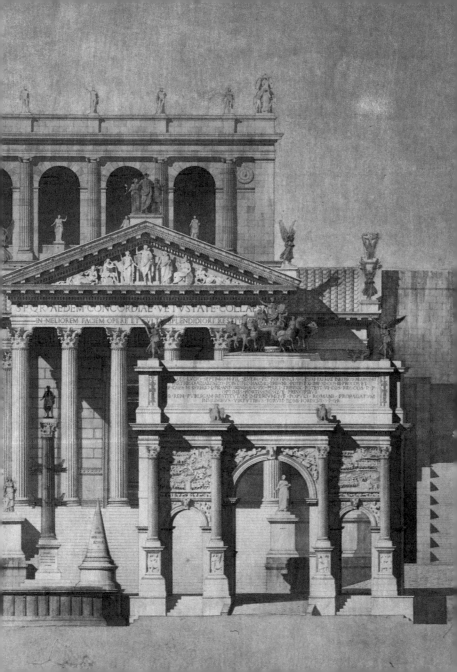

SPQR AEDEM CONCORDIAE VETVSTATE COLLAP
IN MELIOREM FACIEM OPERE ET CVLTV SPLENDIDIORE RESTITV

BASILIQUE DE L'IMLEE

TABVLARVM

MONT

CAPITOL.

TEMPLE DE LA CONCORDE

TEMPLE DE VESPASIEN

TEMPLE
DE JUPITER TONANT

E SATVRNE

ROCHE TARPÉIENNE

CONTENTS

I ROME, THE ETERNAL CITY
13

II THE AGE OF THE HUMANISTS
29

III FROM PRIVATE COLLECTIONS TO ART HISTORY
59

IV ROME UNDER NAPOLEON
85

V THE AGE OF REASON
101

VI FROM ONE MYTH TO ANOTHER
121

DOCUMENTS
145

Further Reading
200

List of Illustrations
200

Index
204

IN SEARCH OF
ANCIENT ROME

Claude Moatti

DISCOVERIES

HARRY N. ABRAMS, INC., PUBLISHERS

In spite of being destroyed and buried time
and time again over the centuries, Rome
never disappeared entirely. The Eternal City—
a great intellectual, political, and artistic
capital—has survived, though the veil of legend
has covered its ruins.

CHAPTER I
ROME, THE
ETERNAL CITY

The *Dittamondo*, by
14th-century author
Fazio degli Uberti, is an
account of an imaginary
voyage. Fazio and his guide,
the ancient geographer
Solinus, arrive at the banks
of a river, where they
encounter an old, weeping
woman (opposite, detail);
she is Rome, the city
personified, and she tells the
poet her story and about her
former beauty.

Right: A 5th-century
depiction of Rome.

As in so many other ancient cities, Rome's history has been obscured. Even in ancient times, buildings were constructed on top of each other: The Baths of Trajan were built over the ruins of the Domus Aurea (Golden House), Nero's palace; the Baths of Diocletian were built on top of two temples and several public and private buildings.

Strolling through the city in the 16th century, the French philosopher and essayist Michel de Montaigne remarked that he knew that he was walking "over the roofs of entire houses" and "on top of the old walls."

Two centuries later the German poet Johann Wolfgang von Goethe (1749–1832) walked through the Campo Vaccino noting that the ancient Roman Forum, surrounded by all kinds of buildings, had become cow pasture; here and there half-buried ruins

F. Chauveau fe.

appeared. (Archaeologists would not clear it until the following century.)

"The hills rise above the rubble," wrote Frontinus, the administrator of the aqueducts in the 2nd century AD. Before the end of the Roman Empire in the 5th century, the physical remains of earlier epochs—royal Rome and republican Rome—had already practically disappeared, covered by more recent construction, which in turn was destined to meet with a similar fate.

For over a thousand years, since the end of the empire, ancient Roman remains have been reemerging gradually from layers of rubble and soil more than twenty yards thick in some places.

In the 12th century, when the struggle between the empire and the papacy had reached its height, the traditional belief that Emperor Constantine had offered the empire to Pope Sylvester—thereby giving him a legitimate foundation for the political power of the popes—was revived. A series of 12th-century frescoes in the Oratory of St. Sylvester illustrates this event: In this example (opposite) Constantine is presenting the crown to the pope.

The invasion of Rome in AD 410 by Alaric the Visigoth terrified pagans and Christians: "It is the end of the world," lamented St. Jerome, "words fail me, sobs prevent me from speaking.... The city that once subjugated the universe has fallen in its turn."

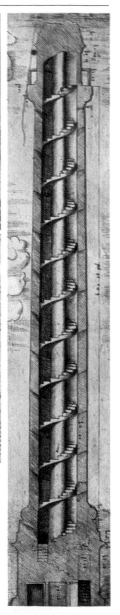

CIRCI MAXIMI et PALATII MAIORIS ut hodie visuntur RELIQVIÆ

PIRAMIS AVT SEPVLCHRVM C·CESTII PROPE PORTÃ S·PAVLI

Rome Robbed of Its Treasures: Rome Destroyed

Burial was not the only way ancient Roman architectural treasures disappeared. The city's riches were also forcibly removed. In the 4th century AD Rome was losing its status as capital of the empire. The new capitals, Constantinople, and later Milan and Ravenna, were each in turn adorned with Rome's riches, taken by the emperors.

General impoverishment and invasions by Germanic

and other groups accelerated the damage. The inhabitants no longer kept up the buildings, the statues and cult objects that were spared by the invaders were dispersed, and the ancient sites—the Forum, the Palatine Hill, the Colosseum—gradually became public refuse dumps or became overgrown or covered with the dust of time.

Some rulers and some invaders, however, were impressed with the monuments that were still visible and attempted to protect them. The Eastern Roman emperor Constantius II, son of Constantine the Great, who would himself strip Rome of a large number of bronzes, was overwhelmed when he made a pilgrimage to the Eternal City in 357. He was fascinated by Trajan's Forum, with its sculpted column and its basilica, and by the markets that stood on the slopes of the Quirinal Hill. He felt that he was looking at "the sanctuary of the world." Theodoric I, king of the Visigoths and ruler of Italy in the late 5th century AD, had Pompey's Theater repaired and encouraged the restoration of the baths, circuses (arenas), sewers, and aqueducts.

From the Pagan City to the Christian City: Pillage and Reuse

After the conversion of Emperor Constantine in around AD 312, Rome became Christian. Pagan worship was banned, and temples were closed by decree at the end of the 4th century. Some temples eventually became churches: The Pantheon, built by Agrippa (son-in-

Opposite: The Circus Maximus in a 17th-century engraving (above); the Meta Remi (below), a funerary monument built at the end of the 1st century BC; and a cross section of Trajan's Column (right) in a 16th-century engraving.

The opening to the sky in the dome of the Pantheon (below) measures almost thirty feet across. An elevation of the Pantheon in a 17th-century drawing (bottom).

The drawings of Maerten van Heemskerck were produced between 1532 and 1536, following Charles V's sack of Rome. The artist has become a precise and realistic observer: He does not guess about the former state of the monuments or invent a reconstruction. The Colosseum really did look like this in the 16th century.

law of Augustus, the first Roman emperor), was consecrated as early as 609 to St. Mary of the Martyrs; the Curia—where the senate met, in the Forum—was dedicated to St. Adrian.

The urban landscape at large was rapidly being transformed. Exhausted by wars, famines, and epidemics, people had abandoned the hills and taken refuge along the Tiber. For several centuries Rome's densely populated center was surrounded by vast abandoned spaces overgrown with vegetation.

Finally, beginning in the 11th century, the ancient buildings that were still intact were taken over and fortified by noble families. The others—temples, baths, and theaters in varying states of disrepair—were used as quarries for marble, a rare and desirable building material. Most often it was sent to the limekilns to be burned and reused. In fact, throughout the Middle Ages, until the Renaissance, thousands of statues and fragments of marble were burned in smoky shops set up between the Capitoline Hill and the Tiber: A street name there has preserved the memory of the destruction, the Via delle Botteghe Oscure, the "street of dark shops."

In the 19th century the archaeologist Rodolfo Lanciani (1847–1929) uncovered limekilns in the Forum, located on site, as it were, which made them most efficient. On the Palatine Hill he found a ditch full of statues, "some charred, others intact," that had been spared for some unknown reason. When it was not burned, the marble of the statues, wall coverings, and columns was sent to Naples, Pisa, Orvieto, Monte Cassino, St.-Denis in France, or even Westminster in England.

All this plunder gave the ruins their present appearance. During the empire Rome had been a city of gleaming marble.

For pilgrims Rome was the most important of all cities, the center of the world. The map below, from the *Einsiedeln Itinerary,* portrays the city as a perfect circle and illustrates the most famous routes. The most important one goes from the Vatican, upper left, across the river to the Lateran, bottom.

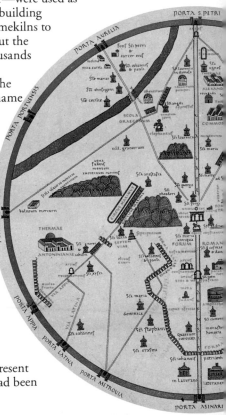

Rome Reborn Again and Again

Yet the buried and broken city never disappeared completely. The Colosseum, the Pantheon, and Trajan's Column have endured through the centuries. Rome has always retained a breath of life, and its "rebirths" were suffused with emotion. In spite of the hostility of the Christians to paganism, the study of Roman history and traditions was not interrupted from the 1st century BC until the Middle Ages. Even then a familiarity with the ancient culture survived in some quarters, and a profound respect was held for its ruins.

The Earliest Guides to Rome Mention the Pagan Monuments

Christian Rome attracted visitors from France, Spain, and Germany just as pagan Rome had. Crowds of pilgrims came to visit the tomb of St. Peter (located in what was originally Nero's Circus), the churches containing the relics of other saints, and the ancient ruins close by. More than two million came in 1300, the jubilee year, when it had been rumored that anyone who visited St. Peter's would receive full absolution.

Guides written especially for these travelers to Rome proposed various tours. One of the oldest and most famous of these, dating from the 8th or the 9th century and known as the *Einsiedeln Itinerary* (because the manuscript was discovered in the Einsiedeln monastery in

Nicolas Poussin's drawing of a statue of Marcus Aurelius.

"In front of the pope's palace, the Lateran, there is a bronze statue: The horse is huge, and his rider, whom some people think is Theodoric, is believed by Romans to be the Emperor Constantine; for the cardinals and the clerics of the Roman Curia, however, he is Marcus or Quintus Quirinus.... The rider is sitting erect; he is leading the people with his right hand and holding the reins in his left hand."
Master Gregorius

Switzerland), offers pilgrims eleven walks through the city. It gives a detailed description of the city walls and enumerates the towers, battlements, windows, and even latrines.

The *Einsiedeln Itinerary* combines a sound knowledge of the city with a special interest in the inscriptions— texts that the ancients engraved on monuments. (The study of inscriptions was a major field in the renewal of classical studies that, as a result of Charlemagne's influence, was taking place at the time.)

The *Mirabilia*, the Cult Books of Medieval Tourism

The *Einsiedeln Itinerary* was only one of many guides for pilgrims called *Mirabilia Urbis Romae (Marvels of Rome)* which had been published for centuries. By the 12th century the *Mirabilia* reflected a decline in the understanding of the city. Direct knowledge of texts and places was obscured by legends and symbols.

Antiquity had acquired a mythological dimension; the ancients appeared to be inimitable giants who had adorned their city with the greatest wonders. In the 12th century Canon Benedict, a cleric at St. Peter's while Innocent II was pope, described these extraordinary works to his contemporaries. By studying ancient texts, Benedict attempted to find the ancient names of the monuments; these names had long been obscured by medieval nomenclature. But his commentary included all the legends and errors of the Middle Ages: He wrote, for example, that the demigods Castor and Pollux were "two young

The title page of one of the 16th-century *Mirabilia* (left).

philosophers who had come to Rome in the time of Tiberius," and that, in the Forum, "there is the Temple of Vesta, beneath which it is said that a dragon lies." He imagined that marvelous palaces resplendent with gold and silver had stood on the Capitoline Hill.

In the 12th century the Romans were demanding their independence from the papacy; while the popes and the Germanic emperors conceived competing plans for a universal Roman-style empire with Rome as its center, the Romans dreamed of an Italy united under them, a new republic built on the pattern of the ancient one. The ancients were admired as highly as ever, and their influence continued to grow.

The *Mirabilia* reflected the desire of the time to revive the consuls and senators, hoping to resuscitate the splendor of the city. These books were very popular. Copied again and again, distributed, and imitated until the 16th century, they set the style of topographic description for a long time to come and gave a lasting account of what was known about Roman monuments. In the 14th century the Italian poet Petrarch derived all that he knew about the city from these guides.

Master Gregorius, Enamored of Venus

Among the most famous *Mirabilia*, the work of Master Gregorius holds a truly special place: An English theologian, Gregorius was a true lover of antiquity who did not hesitate to criticize destructive and iconoclastic popes. When he arrived in Rome he was fascinated from the very first glimpse by this city's many towers, narrow streets, and innumerable churches. The walks he took increased his admiration: He saw pyramids, arches, and monumental

Left: In the Middle Ages some people believed that this colossal head of the emperor Constantine represented the sun-god.

Above: Emperor Frederick II (1194–1250) was extremely knowledgeable about ancient Rome, and he encouraged Classical studies. In Sicily he established the first medieval codification of the administrative laws of state, which were inspired by the Roman code of the emperor Justinian.

buildings, or palaces. He was delighted by everything, especially the statues. Their beauty seemed to him to come from a magical power. One in particular fascinated him, a Venus "which is so indescribably perfect that she almost seems to be alive; like a girl blushing at her own nudity, her face grows red." Gregorius went back to see her three times, in spite of the long walk he had to take to get there.

Gregorius was not a scholar, even though he claims that he was not taken in by all the stories pilgrims were generally told. But he lived in the Middle Ages, and his observations reflect a time when Rome had become a confusing labyrinth, a forest in which travelers could get lost. It was a time when a taste for legends had taken the place of every other form of understanding. The Pantheon was believed to have been the home of demons; the Colosseum, the Temple of the Sun. In fact, Gregorius pointed the way to 14th-century humanism, both by his sense of pure beauty and by his ability to be moved by a statue.

A Time of Tension and Turmoil

This was a period of tension, marked by a series of challenges to papal authority. In 1309 Philip IV of France forced the relocation of the papacy to Avignon. During the popes' exile, which lasted until 1378, most Italian cities were experiencing a strong national awakening stimulated by a revival of interest in ancient culture.

The political renaissance of Rome seemed to favor archaeological research: Excavations were organized, and vases, pottery, and statues found at various sites drew great attention. Emperor Frederick II (who ruled from 1215 to 1250) organized the exploration of the ancient Greek city near Augusta,

the city he had founded in 1232. Of course, people's interest in marbles and statues during this period was primarily to trade in them. Admirers of antiquities were treasure hunters, and the respect for some works, especially tall bronze statues, was partly motivated by the inability to make similar ones at the time.

Cola di Rienzo, a Tribune of the People, and the Nostalgia for Republican Rome

A young Roman by the name of Cola di Rienzo (1313–54), who was a friend of Petrarch's and a defender of the people against the abuses of the nobles, "spent whole days examining the marble sculptures that littered the ground in Rome," according to his anonymous biographer. Apparently, nobody could read the ancient epitaphs as well as Cola di Rienzo: He could explicate all the ancient inscriptions and interpret correctly all the figures of marble.

In 1346 Rienzo discovered a bronze plaque engraved with the law bestowing imperial powers on Emperor Vespasian (ruler from AD 69 to 79). It had been used in the altar of the Basilica of the Lateran, built probably in the 4th century. For centuries, the inscription had faced inward. A fire in the basilica finally led to its discovery and deciphering.

Rienzo displayed the document and assembled the people. Already well known for his antiaristocratic feelings, he explained: "Sublime Rome lies in the dust, she cannot see her own fall since the emperor and the pope have torn her very eyes out. Romans, see how great was the magnificence of the senate that conferred the

NICOLO DI LORENZO DETTO COLA DI RENZO, Tribuno del Popolo Romano.

If the 14th-century Italian poet Petrarch (opposite, painted by Andrea del Castagno) was to be considered by posterity to be the incarnation of the renewal of Classical literature, Cola di Rienzo (above), at first, personified the desire to revive the political forms of antiquity. Later he became a tyrant and finally was killed during a popular uprising. He was dragged through the streets of the city for three whole days; his body was beaten, stoned, dismembered, and then burned.

empire on this individual!"

The people of Rome listened attentively. In 1347 Rienzo was elected tribune of the people. He spoke on the very spot where the Gracchi, Cicero, and the Caesars had once aroused the crowds' passions.

But this "liberator" who exalted the people, this defender of the communal ideal who reduced the barons to impotence, reformed the city-state, and strove for Italian unity, slowly became a terrible tyrant. He was deposed and imprisoned. When he was called back to resume his authority, his excesses became even more outrageous. Finally, he was tortured and put to death.

From the Scholars of the Middle Ages to the Renaissance Humanists

Rienzo was the last person of his time to call for the restoration of Rome while cherishing his great love of scholarship and his understanding of the monuments, literary texts, and inscriptions.

His contemporary Giovanni Dondi, a philosopher, physician, and astrologer, really belonged to the age of humanism. In Dondi's *Iter Romanum*, a collection of notes taken in the course of his journey to Rome, he gives the precise dimensions of the monuments and avoids repeating mere legends.

Dondi's approach to antiquity is unemotional: He does not appeal to magic, to political exaltation, or to poetry. His encounter with Rome relies on figures and texts. It was his critical spirit that led him to express his admiration for what he found.

This 1st-century bronze tablet (above) conferring imperial powers on Emperor Vespasian was discovered by Cola di Rienzo in 1346 in the altar of the Basilica of the Lateran.

Rome is portrayed as a lion in this late-13th-century drawing (opposite). Cola di Rienzo, too, said: "The walls of the city form the outline of a lion at rest."

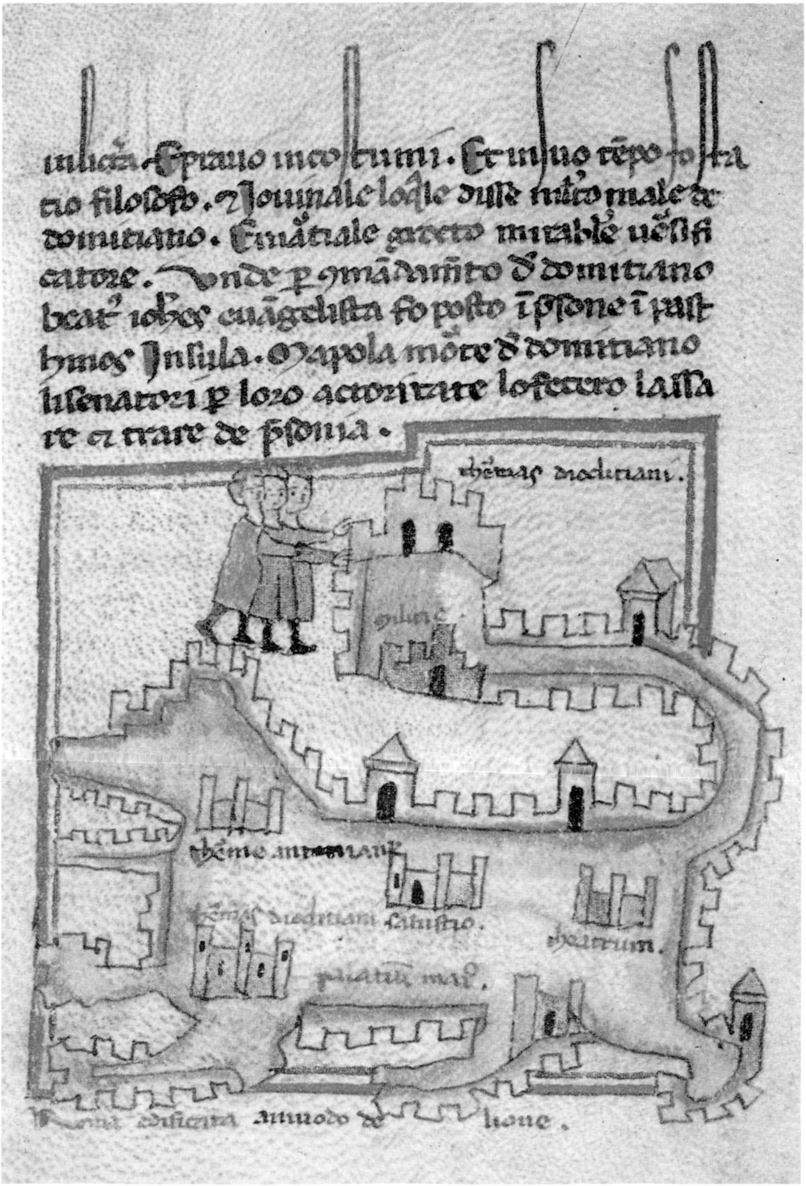

While Christopher Columbus was exploring the New World, artists, scholars, princes, adventurers, and popes were searching feverishly through the soil of Rome for the remains of its former splendor. Rome was being plundered; brought back to life in descriptions, maps, and plans; and actually rebuilt—all at the same time.

CHAPTER II
THE AGE OF THE HUMANISTS

The Laocoön Group (opposite, in a room in the Domus Aurea, where it was discovered) is "an artistic wonder, in which the greatest beauty is born of the greatest suffering," according to German archaeologist Johann Joachim Winckelmann.

This miniature map of Rome comes from the Limbourg brothers' *Les Très Riches Heures du Duc de Berry* (15th century).

In the 15th century the city was dirty, depopulated, and completely in ruins; a contemporary description compared it to an old woman dressed in rags. The great historian Gian Francesco Poggio Bracciolini (1380–1459) saw in Rome the symbol of humanity, subject as it was to the vagaries of fortune.

In what was a genuine challenge to time, antiquarians, those learned in ancient matters, undertook to restore both the city's identity and its unity.

In addition, great projects to care for public works were organized by the popes. Because of their overwhelming passion for collecting masterpieces from the pagan past, the popes were even accused of heresy on the eve of the sack of Rome by the troops of Charles V in 1527.

More than anything else, however, it was the insatiable intellectual fervor of the period that was responsible for the beginnings of archaeological research. As the great explorers set sail for new continents, scholars, artists, and princes set off in search of Rome.

A bove the statue of Marcus Aurelius (above right), the hand and head of a colossal statue designate the Lateran as a place of justice and the political power of the popes. At the end of the 15th century and the beginning of the 16th, these bronze artifacts were moved to the Capitol, where they still remain. These four miniatures are taken from the 15th-century *Codex Mutinesis.*

M onte Testaccio (above left), a hill formed of fragments of pottery, marking an ancient commercial site.

Scholarly Walks

Cyriacus of Ancona (1391–1452), a merchant and dealer in antiquities, walked or rode his white horse through the city every day "in search of remains, temples, theaters, palaces, and baths, splendid obelisks, arches, aqueducts, bridges, statues, columns, and noble inscriptions. He examined them, transcribed them, and commented upon them"; he wanted to revive the dead and reveal their identity. In his *Itinerary,* he tells of his expeditions to Italy, Egypt, Greece, and Palestine. He includes numerous previously unpublished texts he had copied and large numbers of monuments he had drawn.

Like Cyriacus, other scholars of the period were enthusiastic walkers. Poggio Bracciolini, for one, ventured to the outskirts of Rome; Julius Pomponius Laetus (1425–98) walked indefatigably around the city. As had Dondi, a century earlier, he collected the notes he took in the course of his walks and produced one of the best topographical commentaries of his time.

Symbols of Rome are placed among imaginary monuments and antiquities: above left, an obelisk with a globe in front of two buildings—clearly St. Peter's and the Castel Sant' Angelo—and, above right, one of the city gates, a bridge, and the Castel Sant' Angelo.

Philology's Finest Hour

The scholars' passion for exploration was directed
first toward manuscripts. These learned people
traveled all over Europe, searching monasteries for
them and copying and translating the texts they
found. Pope Nicholas V (who reigned from 1447
to 1455) never went anywhere without his army of
scribes. At the time of the fall of Constantinople,
Nicholas ordered his agents to acquire Greek
manuscripts regardless of their cost. For the eight
years of his papacy, he expanded the collections of
the Vatican library, which, with its five thousand
volumes, became the first great library of Europe. His
scholars, including Poggio Bracciolini, began to translate
and explicate texts in order to establish sound editions
from the variants found in the different manuscripts.

Among the Roman authors rediscovered at the time

One of the reading
rooms of the
Vatican library at the
beginning of the 17th
century (above).

were Ovid, Livy, Lucretius, Statius, Quintilian, and, most significantly, the 1st-century writer Vitruvius. Vitruvius' treatise, *De Architectura,* would influence both the architecture of the Renaissance—for example, in the work of Andrea Palladio (1508–80)—and the understanding of the ancient monuments. With the aid of mathematical instruments he had invented, the architect Leon Battista Alberti (1404–72) measured the ancient buildings and produced precise descriptions of them in accordance with Vitruvius' classifications. Alberti's *Description of Rome* includes drawings and figures of many monuments as well as analyses of their structure.

Saving the Memory of Stone

Philology, the study of ancient language and literature, went hand in hand with a systematic search for inscriptions—dedications of monuments, funerary texts, laws, and senatus consulta (decrees of the Roman senate). Bernardo Rucellai's work, *De Urbe Roma,* for example, brought descriptions and inscriptions together. Scholars hurriedly made tremendous efforts to save the memory made of stone, with a haste and passion reflecting their legitimate fear of seeing its last traces disappear, as new monuments were still being built with stones taken from the old ones. In 1430 Poggio Bracciolini began a series of *sylloges*—collections of pagan and

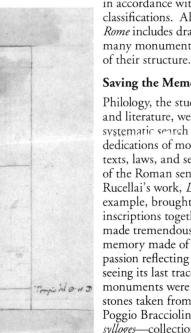

Tempio del O· et D

This illuminated manuscript is from the 14th century.

"Among the copyists, those who knew Greek occupied the front row; there were only a few of them and they were paid well.… At the time of Nicholas V, most of the copyists in Rome were Germans and Frenchmen: They were called barbarians by the Italian humanists."
  Jacob Burckhardt, (1818–97), *The Civilization of the Renaissance in Italy*

Opposite: For centuries Venus had occupied a very important place in the Roman pantheon. Rome did not become a divinity protecting the empire until the reign of Emperor Hadrian (AD 117–38). At this time the Temple of Venus and Rome—the colonnades of which dominated both the Forum and the Colosseum—was regarded as the religious and political center of the state. By the 15th century the building was a ruin; this drawing of it by Andrea Palladio shows an idealized view rather than an archaeological reconstruction.

Christian inscriptions. *Sylloges* proliferated in subsequent centuries with the help of the printing press and the enthusiasm of numerous publishers.

All these collections, which scholars in the 18th and 19th centuries took the trouble to classify, reveal a widely shared determination to bring together as many documents as possible. The haste of collecting caused some problems: The dates of discoveries were often not noted, places where fragments were found, and their dimensions, were often not specified. Sometimes data were entirely invented.

Humanist Scholarship—a Heresy?

In his house on the Quirinal Hill, Julius Pomponius Laetus amassed inscriptions, coins, and fragments of marble; together with his friends and disciples he founded the Roman Academy, an association of enthusiasts and scholars. At their meetings they ate sumptuous banquets in the ancient style. Sometimes they assembled in the catacombs (subterranean burial vaults of the Early Christians), where one can still find the graffiti they left. Every member assumed an ancient name: Pomponius took the name of Pontifex Maximus,

which was both the title of the head of the Roman religion in ancient times and the Latin translation of *pope.*

When word of their meetings reached Pope Paul II, he became worried that Pomponius was a heretic who was organizing pagan banquets for his friends. Was he plotting some kind of conspiracy? In 1468 twenty members of the society were arrested and put in chains in the

Originally the mausoleum of Emperor Hadrian, the Castel Sant' Angelo (above) was transformed into a fortress in the 3rd century AD, when it was incorporated into the great Aurelian Wall. Its defenses were continually reinforced until the 16th century. During the sack of Rome in 1527 Pope Clement VII took refuge there by using the fortified corridor that linked it with the Vatican.

Adversaries Julius Pomponius Laetus (left above), an Italian humanist, and Pope Paul II (left below).

dungeon of the Castel Sant' Angelo. Pomponius wrote a defense and protested his innocence. What followed was one of the first trials in modern history in which humanist scholarship was equated with paganism. It prefigured the accusations that were made against the church a century later during the Reformation.

There was no proof of the guilt of the scholars, who were nonetheless accused of every vice. (The meetings in the catacombs and the graffiti remained secrets.) Pomponius was released. Immediately, he resumed his lectures at the university, and they were so popular students arrived before midnight to reserve their seats. Pope Sixtus IV, who succeeded Paul II in 1471, even allowed Pomponius to revive the academy, which was later joined by a large number of scholars, including statesman Conte Baldassare Castiglione and Cardinal Pietro Bembo. Finally, however, the sack of Rome in 1527 led to the academy's being dissolved: It was considered dangerously pagan.

The Birth of Literary Topography

Pomponius' knowledge of the ancient monuments placed him among the greatest experts in this field at a time that saw the coming of the age of topography, the analysis of the structures and features of the ancient city. In the 15th century attempts were made to restore the ancient place names that had been

At times, ancient literary texts and inscriptions refer to each other: The bronze tablet below, discovered in 1528, reproduces Claudius' speech to the Roman senate on behalf of the Gauls; a century later Tacitus mentions the speech in his *Annals*.

obscured by the Middle Ages, and to rediscover the reality that lay behind the medieval legends. Poggio Bracciolini, Bernardo Rucellai, and especially Flavio Biondo were the first to compare texts with inscriptions and remains. The very title of Biondo's book *Roma Instaurata (Rome Restored)* revealed the aim of these new topographers: to rebuild Rome by scholarly evocation, which was just as important as physical restoration. Biondo's second book, *Roma Triumphans,* was a treatise on Roman antiquities. He was fond of the ruins and, above all, an admirer of modern and Christian "triumphant" Rome; its greatness seemed to him to extend that of the ancient city.

For the topographers of the 15th century, ancient literature was more important than any other source.

"The artist may be inspired by wild flowers...or by other motifs that are called grotesques.... This name does not suit them, since ancient artists enjoyed imagining monsters that combined the forms of goats, cows, and mares. By combining different forms of foliage, they created different types of monsters; monsters is, in fact, their true name, and it suits them much better than grotesques."
Benvenuto Cellini
(1500–71)
Autobiography

Paintings (grotesques) from a Vatican loggia copied from ancient Roman decorations.

Archaeology was still not a science. There were no scientific excavations, only individuals rummaging about looking for treasures in the soil. The only written

accounts of major discoveries were produced by amateurs and were only picturesque catalogues devoid of historical analysis. Similarly, artists were looking for models. They depicted ruins in the state in which they found them rather than excavations in progress. It was not until the end of the 16th century that the first reliable accounts of excavations began to appear.

This reproduction of a richly painted vault from the Domus Aurea is by Pietro Santi Bartoli, a 17th-century artist.

Roman Artists Were Ecstatic When They Saw the Grotesques of the Domus Aurea

At the beginning of the 16th century, laborers working near the Colosseum penetrated the basements of a building whose vaults were adorned with frescoes and stuccos. This was the Domus Aurea (Golden House), a huge palace built by Emperor Nero over the remains of a building that had burned down. The Domus Aurea had been covered over shortly after Nero's death in AD 68 by the Baths of Trajan. It was some time before the imperial residence was identified.

The Domus Aurea galleries, which were thought to have been underground from the very beginning, were called grottoes, and their mural paintings of ornamental designs and mythological figures were called grotesques.

The discovery of the grotesques was to have a profound

Julius II, pope from 1503 to 1513, shown here in a portrait by Raphael, claimed descent from the family of Julius Caesar.

The discovery of *The Laocoön Group* (below) in 1506 affected all artists, who eagerly copied what they considered to be *the* masterpiece of ancient art. This mid-16th-century drawing (left) is by Federico Zuccari. Recent discoveries made in Sperlonga, south of Rome, suggest that *The Laocoön Group* was not an original Roman statue but a marble copy of a Hellenistic work made of bronze.

influence on the artists of the Renaissance, who began to decorate palaces with imitations of them. One of the greatest, Raphael (1483–1520), also drew inspiration from them when decorating the loggias in the Vatican Palace. Even more important was the fact that the frescoes provided the first color illustrations of antiquity: The mural paintings of Pompeii and Herculaneum were not discovered until two centuries later.

The Laocoön Group, "Masterpiece of the Arts," Aroused Everyone's Desire

The Domus Aurea contained inexhaustible riches. In 1547 alone twenty-five statues were discovered there; but the greatest discovery had been made earlier, in 1506, when the owner of the land discovered statuary representing two children and their father being strangled by a serpent: This was *The Laocoön Group*, which Pliny the Elder (AD 23–79) had called the masterpiece of the arts. Sent to inspect it by Pope Julius II, both architect Giuliano da Sangallo (1445–1516) and Michelangelo confirmed Pliny's judgment. This marvelous work seemed, as a contemporary wrote, "to exude the scent of immortality." Pope Julius acquired it and had it moved to the Belvedere court in the Vatican, in what was truly a triumphant procession.

The fame of *The Laocoön Group* became so great

that, after the Victory of Marignano in 1515, Francis I, the king of France, claimed it as one of his spoils of war. Pope Leo X (Julius' successor in 1513) refused to part with the original and secretly had a copy of it made; but neither the original nor the copy ever reached the French king. Much later, in 1797, *The Laocoön Group* was carried off by Napoleon as a spoil of war, but it was restored to the Vatican after his defeat.

The First Collections of Antiquities Were Kept at the Belvedere Court and on the Capitoline Hill

The Laocoön Group joined another pagan statue at the Belvedere, an exquisite Apollo. Leo X added others that were found behind the Pantheon. The collection thus grew rapidly, in spite of the reluctance expressed by some popes to acquire ancient pagan art. Adrian VI (1522–3) and Pius V (1566–72), for example, were hostile to ancient culture. They locked the doors of the museum and even sold some of the statues inside.

The Belvedere held only one collection of ancient art. On 18 January 1471, in the Palazzo dei Conservatori on the Capitoline Hill, Pope Sixtus IV had opened to the public the first large collection of antiquities. There people were able to discover the *Spinario* (or *A Boy Picking a Thorn from His Foot),* probably from the 1st century BC, the archaic *She-Wolf,* and the *Lion Devouring a Horse.* Innocent VIII later had the colossal head of Constantine placed there.

These and other ancient statues aroused universal admiration. Princes and wealthy art lovers of Europe had copies made of them. Francesco Primaticcio (1504–70), an Italian painter and architect, was sent to Rome by King Francis I in 1540. He returned with more than a hundred cases of plaster casts and marble pieces he had bought. Philip II of Spain commissioned Diego Velázquez to draw all the statues of the Belvedere, with a view to adorning the royal palace in Madrid with imitations of them.

The Collecting Fashion Proved Useful to Archaeology

Encouraged by these early discoveries, Romans and foreigners began to excavate in earnest, seizing even the smallest fragment of marble.

In every palace, the courtyards and galleries became veritable private museums; whole walls were encrusted with marble reliefs. One

Rome contained no fewer than ninety private collections in the middle of the 16th century. Catalogues of the period, such as Ulisse Aldrovandi's *The Antiquities of the City of Rome,* 1576, enable us to understand how important collecting antique art had become, transforming palaces into museums. In the courtyard above, depicted by Maerten van Heemskerck, one sees an attempt to make use of modern architecture to emphasize ancient statues.

Pope Leo X, 1518, by Raphael (opposite).

The *Apollo Belvedere,* a Roman copy of a Greek statue of the 4th century BC (left).

supremely refined touch was to build one's house in the ruins. Special envoys were sent to Rome from all over Europe to find out about the discoveries and to make purchases; columns, fragments of marble, and statues were thus exported in vast quantities.

This passion of princes and of popes was undoubtedly of great benefit to archaeology. In the 16th century in the Baths of Caracalla (named for the 3rd-century emperor), archaeologists for the Farnese family, leading Roman aristocrats, unearthed some extraordinary treasures: the famous *Hercules,* a colossal statue almost ten feet tall; the group of the *Bull;* a *Flora;* and a number of mosaics.

The nobles of antiquity owned elaborately laid-out gardens, and the excavation of these sites also produced a large number of masterpieces. The *Hercules, Venus, Asclepius,* and the busts of the emperors from the gardens of the Licinii were installed in Pope Julius III's country palace, the Villa Giulia. In 1582 the pictorial group known as the *Aldobrandini Marriage* (named after its owners) was discovered on a wall in the gardens of the Lamia family; this is one of the rare examples of large-scale antique painting. In the gardens of the Sallusti, the largest in antiquity, a colossal goddess' head, most probably a Venus, was found. The statue's throne— the "Ludovisi Throne"—was not discovered until the 18th century.

In the course of these random excavations, in 1562 the first fragments of the Forma Urbis, a marble plan of Rome made between AD 205 and 208, were unearthed. The significance of this discovery was not grasped immediately, but its publication in the next century marked a decisive stage in Roman topography.

Thanks to the Great Construction Projects, Many New Discoveries Were Made

During the building of the Via Leonina (now the Via di Ripetta), large marble fragments of the mausoleum of Augustus were discovered. This imperial tomb had been built at the start of the empire. It was almost totally destroyed in the 12th century and rebuilt and fortified in the 13th century. Close by, in 1568, a part of the

The Forma Urbis suffered much damage from the 5th century on. According to a report by Flaminio Vacca, the first fragments of it were found in May 1562; one is shown at right.

Augustus' tomb (below) consisted of a sort of drum, roughly thirty feet in diameter, topped by a cone of earth planted with trees. The emperor's statue occupies the central bay.

Mausoleum ab Augusto ext...
Mausoleo di Augusto fatto per...

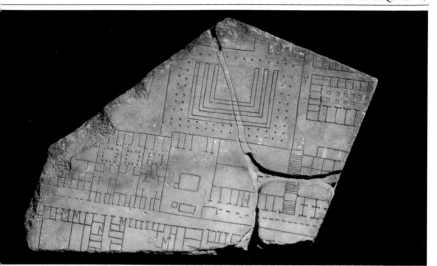

ace, posteris͠qʒ eius sepulti Spectat ad Septemtⁿ Pius·II·Papa Caput S·Andreæ in Basilica S·Petri transferendi solemniter curat Syglio͠
opriu, et de suoi Guarda a Tramontana. Pio·II·Papa fa portar la Testa di S·Andrea a S·Pietro solennemente.

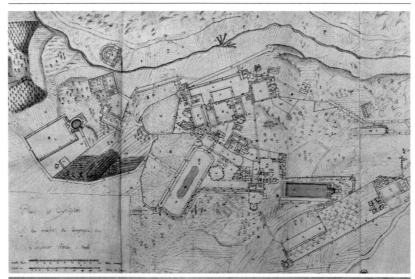

Ara Pacis (Altar of Peace) was discovered. It had been begun in 13 BC and completed in 9 BC, during the golden age of Roman sculpture. The rest of the altar was not discovered until the 19th and 20th centuries.

One of the finest archaeological sites in Italy was the Villa Adriana, or Hadrian's Villa. The emperor Hadrian (AD 76–138) had had a magnificent palace built very close to Tivoli, sixteen miles northeast of Rome. According to a 15th-century visitor, it was "as large as a city," and every part of it bore the name of a famous site in the empire: There was the Lyceum, the Academy, the Canopus, the Poikile, and even the Underworld! In it, one could move from the libraries to the maritime theater, from the gardens to the Temple of Serapis, from large baths to small ones. However, like Nero's Domus Aurea, the villa was abandoned for some time after Hadrian's death and rapidly fell into a state of ruin.

Pirro Ligorio's map (opposite above) reveals the complexity of Hadrian's Villa. Its ruins are shown in this lithograph (above) and watercolor (opposite below).

Pirro Ligorio, Topographer and Antiquarian

Pirro Ligorio (c. 1500–83) was the first to explore the villa. This antiquarian, architect, and topographer had been commissioned by Cardinal Ippolito d'Este to find the materials, marble, ornamental tiling, and works of art for the building of a villa at Tivoli. This utilitarian commission did not prevent Ligorio from undertaking a serious excavation. He documented his work in the *Description of the Superb and Very Rich Villa Adriana.*

Rich mosaics of animals, such as this *Mosaic of the Doves,* were found in Hadrian's Villa.

Ligorio was one of the finest archaeologists of the 16th century. Even though he did not hesitate to fabricate what he did not know, many of his intuitions have since

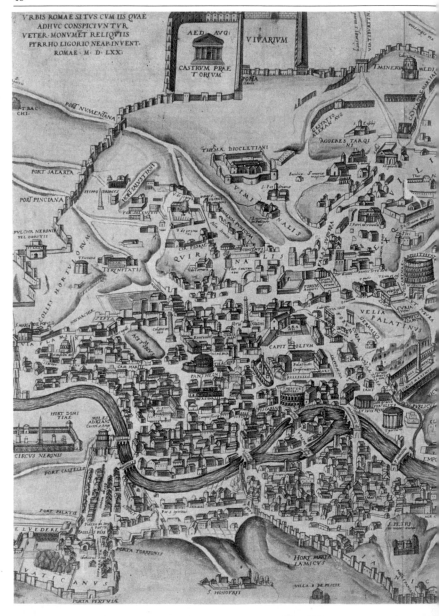

URBIS ROMAE SITUS CUM IIS QUAE
ADHUC CONSPICIUNTUR
VETER·MONUMĒT RELIQUIIS
PYRRHO LIGORIO NEAP·INVENT·
ROMAE·M·D·LXX·

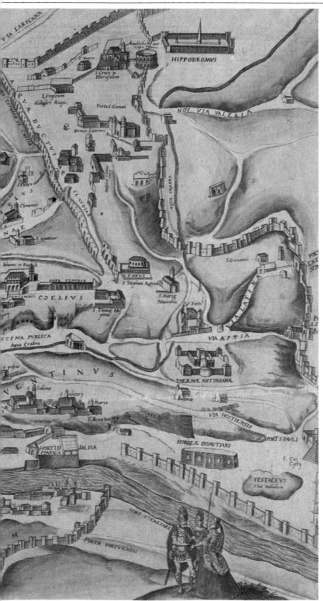

Many maps of Rome were drawn in the middle of the 16th century. Pirro Ligorio's archaeological map (1551), reproduced here, takes the form of a kind of aerial view of the city as seen from the Janiculum, a fortified ridge to the west of Rome. One can make out the principal sites: the Palatine, the Forum, the Capitoline, and the ruins of the ancient monuments.

been proven correct. He personally visited all the sites in Rome where excavations were in progress, and he left reports and plans of his own work. His great talents as an antiquarian, demonstrated by his *Dictionary of Antiquities* and his archaeological map of Rome, led Pope Pius IV to appoint him supervisor of the monuments. In this position he left vivid testimony to the contradictions of his age, divided as it was by an impatience to resurrect the ancient city and a will to modernize it. He proposed that the unearthed remains should be left in place, but he was powerless in the face of the destruction that went on. "As the columns and other parts were revealed," he wrote of the Arch of Augustus, "I saw something that I could not have imagined: Most of the building's ornaments were sold as though in a cattle market.... The epitaphs were lost through ignorance and ill-will and...when I cannot say any more about it, I weep."

R ome's leaders in the 16th century wavered between the protection of the ruins and the modernization of Rome. With Domenico Fontana (1543–1607), his official architect, Sixtus V (above), pope from 1585 to 1590, conceived a construction plan to open wide vistas, to the detriment of the ancient monuments.

A bove left: The building of St. Peter's Basilica, depicted in a fresco by Giorgio Vasari (1511–74).

To Modernize Rome, the Popes Condemned a Large Number of Ancient Monuments

It was indeed an era of destruction, beginning with a brief written on 17 December 1471 by Pope Sixtus IV authorizing the architects of the Vatican library to undertake any excavation they wished, with a view to obtaining stone.

Under Alexander VI (pope from 1492 to 1503) the Holy See put up for auction the Forum and the Colosseum, among other sites.

Apart from the excavations, it was the building of St. Peter's Basilica that caused the greatest amount of destruction. On 22 July 1540 Pope Paul III condemned the Forum. Excavation permits, which had until then been issued jointly by the municipal authorities, the road inspectors, and the Holy See, were granted exclusively and quite freely to the builders of the new basilica. In spite of protests, Pope Gregory XIII (1572–85) affirmed this measure and extended it to the sites

Architect Domenico Fontana in the frontispiece of his *Della Trasportatione dell'Obelisco Vaticano.*

This drawing shows St. Peter's Basilica around 1536. It was completed in May 1590. Modern Rome was gradually being built.

of Ostia and Porto, two of Rome's ancient seaports. Finally, at the end of the century, Pope Sixtus V and his architect, Domenico Fontana, who was responsible for moving the obelisk from the Circus of Nero to its present position in front of St. Peter's, had a number of celebrated remains demolished: A third of the Baths of Diocletian, part of Claudius' aqueduct, the Septizonium of Emperor Septimius Severus, and a large number of Early Christian or medieval buildings were destroyed, including the Patriarchum—the popes' former residence on the Lateran, which had been rich in oratories, chapels, and mosaics—and the fine Oratory of Santa Croce, built in the 5th century by Pope Hilarius. The Oratory had

It took a hundred workers six days to lower the obelisk in the Circus of Nero, and a whole month to move it, with the help of scaffolding and teams of men and animals. This depiction of the event was made at the time.

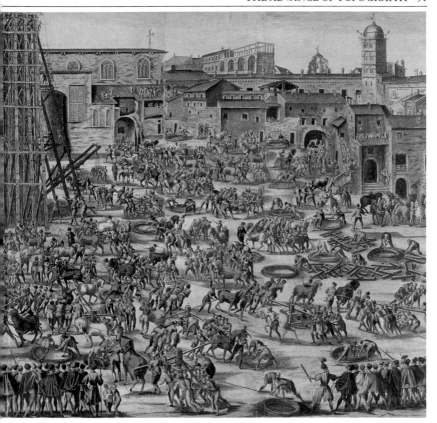

been adorned with a portico, fountains, marble basins, and magnificent golden mosaics.

Despite the destruction, the popes also strove to protect the monuments that were still intact—such as Trajan's Column and Marcus Aurelius' Column—and to limit the exporting of marble and the trade in antiquities.

On 20 August 1515 Raphael, the great painter from Urbino, was made commissioner of antiquities. He was responsible for prohibiting the destruction of inscriptions—a job in which he was not very successful—though his efforts did bring about a genuine improvement in the knowledge of the topography of Rome. The artist chose able collaborators: the epigrapher

Finally, on 10 September 1586, the obelisk was raised in St. Peter's Square, in front of a silent crowd. More than eighty feet high, the monolith was placed on an enormous pedestal and surrounded by four bronze lions.

Jacopo Mazochio and the antiquarians Fabio Calvo and Andrea Fulvio. The team's goal was to draw up an archaeological map of Rome "restored to its ancient form, to its former perimeter, and to the proportions of its different parts." After Raphael's death in 1520 his friends continued his work. In 1521 Mazochio published a collection of inscriptions, and in 1527 Calvo published a map of Rome and Fulvio published his *Antiquities of Rome*.

The Sack of Rome Interrupted the Development of Archaeology for Twenty Years

Shortly afterward, on 6 May, Holy Roman Emperor Charles V's troops occupied and ransacked the city. Fulvio and Calvo perished in the general massacre. This raid, one of the most destructive Rome has ever suffered, marked an interruption in the history of archaeology. A strange silence reigned in the city at the end of 1527 after the raids and acts of sacrilege—a contemporary wrote that "one no longer hears any bell, none of the churches is open, no masses are said anymore."

Studies of Roman topography were finally resumed twenty years later, with the work of Pirro Ligorio and with the discovery of the catacombs.

Unknown Cities Lay Hidden Beneath Rome's Streets and Houses

Fulvio had devoted books IV and V of his work to the Christian basilicas and cemeteries. Before him, Poggio

A portrait of Emperor Charles V by a 16th-century painter.

"I pointed my musket in the direction of a denser and thicker skirmish and I took as my target a soldier who was right in the middle of it and whom I saw dominating others. Turning quickly to Alessandro and Cecchino, I ordered them to fire their muskets and showed them how to dodge the fire of those we were facing. When we had each fired two shots, I looked carefully over the wall and I noticed an extraordinary degree of confusion among the enemy: Our fire had killed [the duke of] Bourbon."
Benvenuto Cellini

1527.
BORBONE OCCISO, ROMANA IN MOENIA MILES
CAESAREVS RVIT, *ET* MISERANDAM DIRIPIT VRBEM.

There is no known contemporary representation of the sack of Rome. This depiction of the battle (left) was made later.

Above: The death of Charles, duke of Bourbon, during the rout, in an engraving by Maerten van Heemskerk.

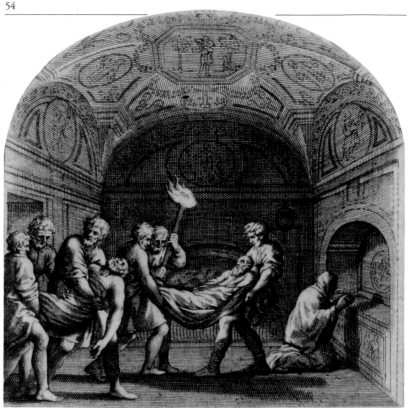

Bracciolini, Cyriacus of Ancona, and Maffeo Vegio (1407–58) had collected Christian inscriptions, but the history of the church did not progress until the second half of the 16th century, when scholars were able to recreate the funerary rites of Early Christians centering on the Oratory of St. Philip Neri. Archaeology was notably absent from their studies. Nearly all of the catacombs still lay buried. In order to revitalize Early Christian history, excavations had to be undertaken, and a new methodology had to be invented.

The engravings on these two pages are from Antonio Bosio's *Underground Rome.*

Nella Naue minore della Porta del Giudit nella base dell'ottaua colonna.

DEPS FELIX DIAC · V· IDVS·MARTIAS
THEODOSIOXV· ETPLD·VALENTINIANOIIII
AAVV.CC·CON· SS.

Bosio, the "Inventor" of the Catacombs

On 31 May 1578, while work was being done in a vineyard bordering on the Via

Salaria, the ground collapsed over an underground cemetery that was decorated with paintings and Greek and Latin inscriptions. It contained sarcophagi.

The preliminary exploration of this site, which attracted thousands of onlookers, was led by the Spaniard Alfonso Ciacconio: He had the paintings he found copied, but his exploration was limited. It was not until several years later that a scholar, Antonio Bosio, revealed the full extent of this discovery.

Bosio was only eighteen years old when he first entered a catacomb in 1593—Domitilla's Catacomb on the Via Ardeatina. Bosio and his friends went bravely into the vast labyrinth in the depths of the earth, attracted by the mystery and silence. The sacred tunnels stretched in long loops in every direction, and the reflections of the candles on the walls made a deep impression on the visitors. Suddenly they found themselves in total darkness. Convinced that they were going to die, they trembled at the idea of despoiling those holy and inviolate places with their dead bodies. They stumbled around for forty-eight hours, until they found a way out. They promised themselves that they would not undertake any further expeditions of this kind without plenty of candles.

This experience confirmed Bosio's dedication to his vocation: From then on he devoted his time to the exploration of the catacombs, reporting his findings in his great book, *Underground Rome* (1632), a description of all the catacombs and the paintings found in them. The topographical order, the constant comparisons made between the excavations, the texts, and the inscriptions all reflect development in the field of Christian archaeology. But Bosio was a man of the 16th century; he lacked a critical method. Nonetheless, one can imagine the excitement aroused by his book, not published until after his death, which presented a picture of Rome as a sacred necropolis.

Bosio's work was used by Catholics and Protestants alike in the dispute about whether the church was faithful to the beliefs and practices of Early Christians. The discovery of the catacombs fueled a controversy that until that time had been based only on texts.

B esides arousing the passion of archaeologists, the Roman ruins stimulated elegiac emotions and offered an ideal setting for genre paintings. In this example one can barely make out the three columns of what was to be identified in the 19th century as the Temple of Vespasian on the right. The charming quality of this scene by Paul Bril (1554–1625) is due to the harmonious unity established between the ruins, nature, and human activities—a sort of contented nonchalance.

I n the 18th century Rome and its remains were in everyone's heart—as a fad, as the favorite subject of artists, as an unforgettable goal of pilgrimage. The mania for antiquity raged throughout Europe. Wealthy collectors began to found museums, and German archaeologist Johann Joachim Winckelmann laid the foundations of art history.

CHAPTER III
FROM PRIVATE COLLECTIONS TO ART HISTORY

R emnants of Roman statuary were a popular subject with 18th-century painters. Opposite: *The Painting Studio* by Michael Sweerts. Right: A painting by Ducros of the *Dioscuri* on the Capitol, one of the most-admired sculptures of the time.

After Bosio, there was a lull in the progress of Christian archaeology: What people sought in the catacombs were relics and treasures. In the 17th and 18th centuries, scholars were busy publishing newly discovered inscriptions and commenting on ancient texts. Jean Mabillon (1632–1707), a Benedictine scholar, rediscovered the *Einsiedeln Itinerary;* Bernard de Montfaucon (1655–1741) published scholarly editions of the works of the church fathers and inventories of the sources of Christian archaeology; Lodovico Antonio Muratori (1672–1750) published a commentary on the Papyri of Monza, which contained a list of the relics that were known at the time of

Gregory the Great (c. 540–604).

The archaeology of the pagan world advanced with the developments of the Renaissance. Great construction projects unearthed gold and silver coins, mosaics, and reliefs; statues, including those of the Temple of Hadrian, were discovered. Papal edicts concerning the control of the excavations had as their main object the expansion of the popes' own collections. Clement XIV decided that discoveries would be divided among four beneficiaries: the pope, the Holy See, the owners of the land, and the people who had financed the projects.

Trade in Antiquities Became Lucrative

Collecting and its natural corollary, trade, remained the primary motivating forces of the "archaeologists": It was in order to sell antiquities or to copy them that Hadrian's Villa (1767) and the Appian Way (1771) were excavated. The restoration of masterpieces also became very lucrative, and scant attention was paid to questions of authenticity. For example, fragments of various statues were put together to form an Apollo, a Venus, or a Diana, depending on the demand. All the foreigners in Rome visited the studio of Bartolomeo Cavaceppi, the most gifted of all the Roman restorers, as if it were a museum.

Most of the buyers were British. In 1732 the Society of Dilettanti, the first association of antiquarians, was founded. This prestigious organization financed the publication of archaeological works and fueled the fashion for a journey to Italy as part of what was known as the Grand Tour. Other Europeans, notably the French and Germans, were influenced by the craze for antiquities. They became passionately interested in Rome and Italy. They bought copies and plaster casts of statues,

Restorer Bartolomeo Cavaceppi (opposite above) perfected a new method of restoration that respected original styles, periods, and materials; it was he who gave restoration its pedigree. *Charles Townley in His Gallery* by Johann Zoffany (above); *A Visit to the Antiquarian* by Jacques Sablet (opposite below).

"The English take everything out of Italy: paintings, statues…. Yet the English hardly ever take anything good."
Baron Montesquieu
18th century

Just as writers collected ancient texts, artists collected antique sculptures and paintings. Giorgio Vasari, the 16th-century art historian, said of one engraver's house that "it was full of so many objects that it was absolutely amazing." These ancient and modern objects included marbles, bronzes, and paintings. Antique art served not only as a model but a source of prestige. By the 17th century this was confirmed: Popes and princes were competing to own the most magnificent collections. This painting, *The Studio of Cornelis van der Geest*, is by Willem van Haecht.

which were cheaper and easier to export than originals. The German poet Johann Wolfgang von Goethe (1749–1832) once proposed that a museum of the inauthentic be created in Rome, in which plaster casts of all the antiquities that had been discovered could be displayed.

The Great Collectors

Renaissance palaces were decorated with antique fragments; in the 18th century, buildings were put up specifically to house gigantic collections. Cardinal Alessandro Albani, a nephew of Pope Clement XI, had the first villa-museum built on the Via Salaria. There he positioned obelisks, columns, sarcophagi, statues, and imperial busts amid bushes, trees, and fountains; reliefs were recessed into the walls of the inner rooms. Daedalus and Icarus, Apollo and Diana, Orpheus and Eurydice lived here. In 1763 architect Carlo Marchionni finished the project: The Villa Albani was said to be a truly fairy-tale residence.

The entrance to the underground ruins of Otricoli (opposite above).

In the middle of the gardens of the Villa Borghese (opposite below) was the Casino, redesigned to house antique statues. It had been built between 1613 and 1615 and was later restored and enlarged. The Asprucci family kept "the queen of private collections" there. Today the grounds of the Villa Borghese (below) comprise the largest public park in Rome, and the Casino is one of its finest museums.

For a Borghese prince, the Villa Pinciana was transformed into a museum of antiquities, and false ruins were created in the immense gardens—a stadium, a Temple of Diana, and a Temple of Asclepius.

Nothing Was Too Beautiful for the Pio-Clementino Museum

Founded by Pope Clement XIV (1767–74) and completed by Pius VI (1775–99), the Pio-Clementino Museum in the Vatican was opened to the public only once a year. Pius VI did not have any concern for·costs: He bought from wealthy

PIVS·VII
P·M·
A·VII

MVSEVM · CL
PIOCLEMENTI

noble collectors or simply appropriated the statues of many buildings, taking the bust of Hadrian and a Minerva from the Castel Sant' Angelo and the sarcophagus of St. Helen from the Lateran. He gave himself preemptive rights over all the discoveries and amassed more than three hundred marbles in the course of his pontificate. Pius VI surrounded himself with talented agents and advisers who catalogued the collection in seven scholarly tomes, confirming the supreme reputation of the Vatican holdings.

Founded by Clement XIV and Pius VI, the Pio-Clementino Museum was enlarged under Pius VII (1800–23) by the creation of the Chiaramonti Museum, of which this fresco is an allegory.

AMONTANVM
· ADIECTVM

The pope organized excavations, especially in Latium, the region surrounding Rome. At Castrum Novum, a former Roman colony, fragments of statues, inscriptions, and gold coins from Nero's reign were discovered. In Salona, also once a colony of Rome, they found the *Venus at Her Bath,* which is now in the Vatican. At Otricoli, forty-five miles north of Rome, an ancient town was almost totally uncovered (including a basilica, theater, and baths).

The present entrance to the Tomb of the Scipios (left) opens onto the most famous Roman road, the Appian Way. In former times the building's facade (shown in an engraving by Giovanni Battista Piranesi, opposite above) faced northwest. Only a small part of it remains today.

The Funerary Rites of the Ancient Romans Became Clearer with the Discovery of the Tomb of the Scipios

In May 1780 several underground chambers containing sarcophagi were discovered in front of the Porta San Sebastiano in Rome. The tomb belonged to the Scipios, a great Roman family that was most famous for having triumphed over the Carthaginians and their leader, Hannibal, in the 3rd century BC.

Visitors were drawn by the tomb's most ancient sarcophagus, that of Barbatus, who conquered the Etruscans in 298 BC. Barbatus' merits are praised in his epitaph: "Lucius Cornelius Scipio Barbatus, the son of Gnaeus, a courageous and wise man; he was a consul, censor, and councillor in your country. He conquered Taurasia and Cisauna, in the Samnium, and subjugated the whole of Lucania, whence he brought back hostages."

When the labyrinth of the tomb was fully explored, it yielded several more sarcophagi, dating between the 3rd century BC and the 1st century AD. Pius VI had the

On the Appian Way, outside the Porta San Sebastiano, the Columbarium of the Emancipated People built by Augustus (below) was a vast structure made up of three adjacent halls containing a thousand niches for urns. Piranesi's engraving conveys the sense of grandeur felt by those who discovered this tomb. In the 19th century other columbaria (vaults with recesses for funerary urns) were discovered along the Appian Way, especially in this area.

sarcophagus of Barbatus and the inscriptions transported to the Pio-Clementino Museum; the other sarcophagi were smashed, the funerary objects were sold, and the bones that were found were dispersed.

In the 17th century it was still believed that, until late in the empire, cremation was the only way Romans had disposed of their dead. This thesis seemed to have been supported in 1777 by the discovery of the *ustrinum* of Augustus, the sacred precinct where the bodies of the emperor and his family and those of his first successors had been burned. But the discovery of the Tomb of the Scipios three years later showed that, from an early date, Romans had also buried their dead.

Further discoveries subsequently confirmed the coexistence of both practices; sometimes there were both urns of ashes and sarcophagi within a single tomb.

The idea of creating gardens on the Palatine Hill occurred to Pope Paul III during the building of the triumphal way in the Forum for Emperor Charles V in 1536. The choice of this hill, where the palaces of the Roman emperors stood, was largely political: It made the pope appear as the true ruler of Rome and its genuine patron. This drawing was made in 1759 by Charles Natoire.

The Palace of Domitian

In ancient times the Palatine
Hill was reserved for the
palaces of the emperors.
This hill had been covered
with vines and pasture since
the Middle Ages, and by
the 16th century only a few
ruins were still visible on it.
In 1535 Pope Paul III had purchased part of the land
and built a splendid villa and garden over the ancient
structures, the remains of which are visible today.
When the Farnese family died out in the late 17th
century, the later dukes of Parma planted bergamot,
vines, and artichokes and feverishly searched for
treasures there. In 1720 Francis I, duke of Parma,
organized a systematic excavation of the site. He
entrusted the responsibility of drawing up the
inventories to Francesco Bianchini, who was
commissioner of antiquities at the time.

Work was confined to the southeastern slope of
the hill, that is, to a part of the former Palace of the
Flavians, built between AD 82 and 96 by Emperor
Domitian. The excavators uncovered three splendid
rooms: the basilica, with its hemispherical vault; the

The Temple of Saturn
(above) surrounded
by houses built in the
18th century.

The coin below, from
the time of
Septimius Severus, shows
a building in the form
of a circus; it is the
Stadium of Domitian
(built at the end of the
1st century AD), the
present Piazza Navona.

throne room, with its sixteen fluted marble columns and twelve niches that held twelve colossal statues of black basalt; and finally, the "lararium." In this room they found a cone-shaped dark stone about three feet high. It has since disappeared. None of the scholars of the time knew what it was. It may have been the Black Stone, a symbol of the goddess Cybele, which was transported to Rome at the end of the 3rd century BC to ward off the Carthaginian threat.

This palace was sumptuous, and it was ransacked rather than excavated: The two ancient yellow marble fluted columns that stood on either side of the door were dispersed; the cornices and sculptures disappeared. The duke of Parma kept two Hercules, a Bacchus, a head of Zeus, and the reliefs for himself. Damage was done to the magnificent frescoes that were found beneath the palace in two rooms dating from an even earlier period:

The Palatine Hill (opposite) was the scene of intense archaeological activity in the 18th century.

the House of the Griffins, so called because of the stucco griffins that formed its decor, and the Aula of Isis, a 1st-century room containing paintings of Egyptian subjects.

The largest of the triumphal arches of Rome, the Arch of Constantine (below, shown during its excavation in the 18th century) stands on the road that leads from the Circus Maximus to the Arch of Titus. It was built by Constantine after his victory at Ponte Milvio in AD 312 to commemorate his mystical vision of the Cross during the battle. For a long time it was difficult to date the arch because of the presence of architectural elements and sculptures of different periods; Constantine had appropriated and reused many different fragments. The eastern slope of the Palatine is also visible in this painting by Abraham-Louis-Rodolphe Ducros.

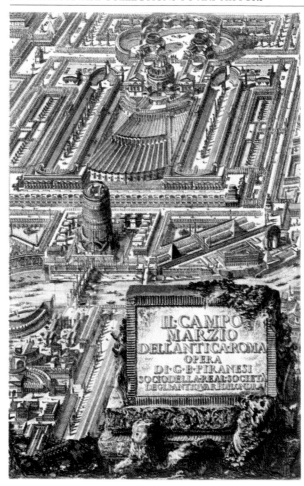

Left: Giovanni Battista Piranesi's bird's-eye-view reconstruction of the area around the mausoleum of Hadrian.

The Painters of the Roman Ruins

While Domitian's palace revealed the baroque nature of Flavian art, the paintings executed earlier in the 1st century AD revealed a more Classical style, which would also be found at Pompeii.

As archaeology became more serious, inventories of the sites, maps, and architectural drawings flourished. They were stimulated by the enthusiasm of publishers

and booksellers. Nicolas Poussin (1594–1665) and other painters of the Classical school focused on ruins, which they treated as elements of a landscape. The success of their *vedute* (views) rivaled that of the traditional engravings. In the debate between the artists who produced drawings of architecture and the landscape painters, the Venetian artist Giovanni Battista Piranesi (1720–78) played a central role. His work brings together all the themes of the period:

Reliquiae Pontis Triumphalis seu Vaticani

Born in Venice in 1720, Piranesi (in profile, above) first studied architecture and then engraving. He moved to Rome around 1740 and stayed there until his death in 1778; in Rome he drew inspiration from the ruins.

The Ravages of Time

The Colosseum was ravaged and used for many purposes: Sixtus V thought of transforming it into a wool mill, and others turned it into a place of devotion—séances were even held there. It was seriously damaged by an earthquake in 1703; Pope Clement XI (1700–21) had the arches filled in with wooden fences, which are visible in this painting by Canaletto (1697–1768). The vegetation on top is authentic.

From a Temple to a Church

These two republican temples located near the Tiber were preserved only because they were transformed into churches: The Temple of Fortuna Virile was given the name Santa-Maria-Egiziaca; the round temple of Hercules became known as Santo Stefano, and later, in 1560, Santa-Maria-del-Sole. In subsequent centuries, both temples were incorporated into modern buildings.

Fragments of Antiques

This *Gallery of Ancient Rome* was painted in 1757 by Giovanni Pannini (1691–1765), a decorator of palaces for the French ambassador to Rome. One finds in this painting most of the great themes of the time: the popularity of the *vedute* (views), decoration, collecting fragments of antique objects, and a sense of playfulness. One is supposed to enjoy identifying the sculptures: on the left, the *Farnese Hercules* and the *Dying Gaul;* on the right, *Spinario,* or *Boy Picking a Thorn from His Foot* and *The Laocoön Group.* Among the monuments: on the left, the Arch of Constantine, the Arch of Titus, and the three columns of the Temple of Vespasian; above, the Pantheon; on the right, the Colosseum.

Views of Rome (1748–78); *Roman Antiquities* (1756), engravings of antique remains; and the *Carceri (Prisons)* of 1745, a kind of fantasy architecture. His maps of Rome, like the works of so many of his predecessors in the 16th and 17th centuries, reflect a genuine passion for remains and fragments. His map of the Campus Martius looks like a fragment of the ancient map of Rome, the Forma Urbis, but Piranesi conveys his own idea of the magnificence of Rome rather than faithfully reconstructing the site itself. In contrast, his map of Hadrian's Villa is of undeniable scholarly value.

New Beginnings: The Birth of the History of Art

Piranesi envisioned a monumental and inventive Roman art, which he defended against the ideas of expert proponents of Greek art as the ultimate expression of antiquity. The quarrel between the champions of Greece and those of Rome was what finally brought archaeology into the modern era.

For the German archaeologist Johann Joachim Winckelmann (1717–68), who had been living in Rome since 1755, Greek art alone had risen to the level of ideal beauty. Thus, "the only means by which we may attain greatness, and if it be possible, to be inimitable, is to imitate the ancients."

Starting with this theory, which was one of the main tenets of the Neo-Classical movement that became fashionable all over Europe, Winckelmann laid the foundations of the first history of art. He described four periods: the Ancient (Archaic Greece), the Sublime (5th century BC), the Beautiful (4th century BC), and the Decadent (2nd and 1st centuries BC and the Roman period).

For Johann Joachim Winckelmann, the "noble simplicity and tranquil grandeur" of Greek art were confirmed by the pure whiteness of the statues.

In this system Rome had little prestige, but this classification did at least make a truly historical approach to the subject possible. Antiquarians and popes had always neglected considerations of history, motivated as they were to accumulate artifacts or to maintain social prestige. Because of Winckelmann, restoration was subjected to strict rules requiring a preliminary study of the styles and precise dating. Thus Winckelmann made ancient art, which had until then only been coveted or imitated, into a subject of historical scholarship, and he made the history of art into one of the main branches of archaeology.

It is an irony of history that Winckelmann, scholarly theorist and admirer of Greek art and author of a *History of Ancient Art,* did not know that a large proportion of the statues he had admired as Greek were, in fact, Roman copies. Yet he founded an entire school, and the discovery of the originals in Greece and Asia Minor was viewed by Winckelmann's disciples as corroborating his new theories.

Born in 1717, the son of a cobbler, Winckelmann (above left) pursued theological and humanistic studies. His passions for mythology and ancient art led him to Rome. He visited the excavations of Herculaneum, Pompeii, and Paestum, and became a friend of Cardinal Albani, who employed him as a librarian. He was assassinated by an unidentified person in 1768.

" The pope will deliver to the French Republic a hundred paintings, busts, vases, and statues chosen by the envoys who will be sent to Rome; these items will include the bronze bust of Junius Brutus and the marble bust of Marcus Brutus, both of which are on the Capitol, as well as five hundred manuscripts to be chosen by the aforementioned envoys. **"**

Article 8 of the Armistice of Bologna

CHAPTER IV
ROME UNDER NAPOLEON

Napoleon's administration showed a constant interest in the Colosseum, clearing and restoring it as well as conducting excavations—shown in this painting by Hubert Robert (opposite)—which yielded many fragments of marble and coins. An 1830 diagram of the Colosseum (right).

The French in Rome, and the Last Great Collection of Roman Art

The French occupation of Rome in the 1790s led to extensive pillaging, which was made legal by the Armistice of Bologna signed by Pope Pius VI and Napoleon Bonaparte. It was confirmed by the Treaty of Tolentino in 1797. As they did in other Italian cities, the French sequestered the great private fortunes, including the rich collections of the Vatican.

Napoleon was in Egypt on 28 July 1799 when the long convoy of the spoils of Rome arrived in Paris in richly ornamented carriages. Canvases by Raphael and Titian, antique manuscripts and sculptures—the *Apollo Belvedere, The Laocoön Group,* and the *Spinario*—and many other marvels made up the collection of antiquities of the French Museum of the Republic. This museum was later renamed the Central Museum of the Arts and was ultimately installed in the Louvre.

Planning and setting up the museum took two years. It opened in November 1801, when 117 works went on display. This was the last great collection made up entirely of Roman art; after the discoveries of the 18th and 19th centuries, objects of more diverse origins were brought together in museums, as in the British

The fresco below by Francesco Hayez evokes the return to Rome of the treasures plundered a few years earlier by the French troops (shown in the engraving above). In the fresco's foreground is a personification of the Tiber River surrounded by *putti* who are looking toward Monte Mario at the arrival of the procession. On the left is a portrait by William R. Hamilton (1777–1859), who played an important role in the recovery of Rome's legacy.

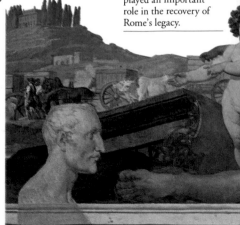

Museum, which held the largest collection of Greek art at the time.

The Treaty of Vienna in 1815 brought about the end of Napoleon's museum, since it included very strict clauses on the subject of restitution. Thanks to the intervention of the Italian sculptor Antonio Canova (1757–1822), the pope recovered almost all his property. Some works were bought by the French, including a large part of the Borghese collection, which formed the core of the Musée Royal, later called the Louvre.

A rchaeologist Ennio Quirino Visconti.

Pius VII and the Legal Protection of the Italian Artistic Heritage

There had been some strong reactions in France to Napoleon's pillaging of Rome. In his *Letters to Miranda,* published during Napoleon's Italian campaign, Quatremère de Quincy, a Frenchman with a passion for

A series of frescoes by different painters commissioned by Antonio Canova (1757–1822) was to illustrate the stages of the restoration of the Italian artistic heritage and the installation of the new collections in the Chiaramonti Museum.

archaeology, recognized the need to safeguard the artistic heritage of Italy. He pointed out how damaging it would be for the works of art to be moved and formulated for the first time the idea that there was an essential relationship between an object and its place of origin.

When Pius VII was elected pope in 1800, he, too, was preoccupied by the question of that heritage. By an edict written in 1802, he banned excavation and export of art objects without papal authorization, obliged individuals to draw up annual inventories of their collections, and granted a budget for the expansion of the museums and the improvement of the teaching of archaeology.

By taking these steps, which were confirmed in 1820 by the Edict of Pacca, Pius VII established the first state protection of artistic heritage, foreshadowing

Architect Quatremère de Quincy (above). Slaves clearing the ruins, 1830 (below).

the gradual disappearance of private collections during the 19th century.

Two men were appointed to implement these decisions: The sculptor Antonio Canova, supervisor of the artistic treasures, was entrusted with the task of inspecting and expanding the museums; Carlo Fea, commissioner of antiquities, was given the role of overseeing the ancient monuments and the churches. Their jurisdiction extended to all of the Papal States, and they were to exert their influence on art and archaeology for more than twenty years.

The Clearing of the Forum Mobilized the Archaeologists

Directed by Carlo Fea, excavations were resumed, principally in the Roman Forum. At the beginning of the 19th century, this was a field crossed by two rows of elm trees and surrounded by isolated houses and stonecutters' shops. Cattle grazed around the half-buried ruins; a huge basin that had been placed near the Temple of Castor and Pollux in 1565 was being used as a water trough.

The archaeologists' main task was to uncover the ruins in order to find the original level of the ground. Then they were to protect the ruins by fencing them off. These measures were applied first to the arches of Constantine and Septimius Severus. One important innovation was that prisoners and slaves took part in these excavations. There were more than a hundred of them at work on the Colosseum; they had cannonballs chained to their feet and were guarded by soldiers.

Yet Pius VII could not afford to begin a genuine program of restoration. The few projects that had been started at the beginning of his pontificate soon slowed down or were suspended as Rome fell into decay and people began to move away from the city. In the opinion

This view of the Forum from the Capitol shows the state of the excavations at the beginning of the 19th century and gives special prominence to the Arch of Septimius Severus, which was uncovered and surrounded by a fence. In the center of the painting, one can see the Column of Phocas and, on the right, the columns of the Temple of Saturn.

of the first secretary of the French Embassy, Rome was on the verge of collapse: "Sitting in the same dust, pagan Rome was sinking into its tombs," he said, "and Christian Rome was gradually going back down into its catacombs."

The Great Excavations Set the Pace of Life in Rome

After it became a "free and imperial city," in 1809, and then a department of the French Empire in August of the same year, Rome, declared by Napoleon to be the second capital of the empire, received large subsidies. At the same time, archaeology was rapidly being transformed. Before, excavations had been conducted sporadically— undertaken for treasure and readily abandoned.

But from this time on, digging was no longer done simply in order to exploit a ruin but to uncover it according to the methods tested by Pius VII. To an even greater extent, restoring huge sites such as Pompeii and analyzing their architectural structures became a goal.

The French undertook large-scale excavations in Rome. These archaeologists were the first to tackle a problem that urban planners have still not resolved: In what way could ruins be allowed to remain a part of the fabric of a modern city? It was said that two cities had to be distinguished: One would have to be modernized and the unnecessary monuments demolished, including some of the churches—there were thought to be too many—and the other would have to be restored by means of extensive excavations.

Official Archaeology Acquired Institutions

The French government began by creating various institutions. The

This portrait of Pope
Pius VII (above) is
by Jacques-Louis David.

The clearing of the
Temple of Vespasian,
known at the time as
the Temple of Jupiter
Tonans (the Thunderer),
was one of the most
spectacular achieve-
ments of the French
administration of Rome.
Above left: The
scaffolding needed in
clearing the architrave.
Left: In these elevations
and plans (insets) one
sees (far left) the capitals
of three columns jutting
out from the earth that
had accumulated at the
foot of the Tabularium
and (near left) the
columns and the large
building on the right that
reappeared after the earth
was cleared away.

Commission for Antique Monuments and Civic
Buildings, founded in 1810 and replaced by the
Commission for the Embellishment of Rome in 1811,
conferred the principal role on the prefect of Rome: He
would issue the permits for excavations, decide the pace
of the projects, and determine the fate of the
objects uncovered.

The teaching of archaeology was also reorganized.
Filippo Aurelio Visconti proposed dividing the subject
into three parts: mythology, the history of art, and
archaeology itself. This third part would be useful to
both artists and historians. Its object, Visconti said,
was "in theory and in practice, to order, interpret,
understand, distinguish, and appreciate antique
works, that is, their period, their value, and what they
represent and signify." Of all the measures taken, this
was the most original.

In this run-down city the French had also found an
impoverished and unemployed population. They decided
to employ the poor on the excavations. Formed into
contingents of a hundred people (men, women, and

Count Pierre Antoine
Daru (1767–1829)
was Napoleon's
representative in Rome.

"The three large arches that we saw occupied the whole length of the nave to the right of the entrance.... The vault was supported by eight thick columns.... The excavations ordered by Napoleon led to the discovery of the floor of this monument; it is made up of violet and cipolin marble."

Stendhal
25 January 1828

children), there were four hundred, and later two thousand, working for the administration.

De Tournon wrote in his *Statistical Studies on Rome* in 1831: "It was thanks to those excavations that an enthusiasm for work spread among the men whose youth had been spent in poverty and indifference toward the future. Initially, there was a scarcity of laborers who were willing to perform what were considered to be the heaviest tasks; but later there was not enough work to employ all those who sought work, such had been the influence of the examples that had been set and so prompt had been the industrial education of the people!"

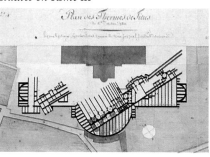

An Exemplary Excavation: the Forum of Trajan

The column that the emperor Trajan had erected in AD 113 to commemorate his victory over the Dacians had survived through the centuries without changing its name or suffering any real damage. The statue of the emperor that had once surmounted it, however, had been replaced

The Baths of Titus (left and above, in an 1811 plan) were covered by the Baths of Trajan, where *The Laocoön Group* was discovered in 1506. Searching for new treasures, more excavations were organized. This led ultimately to the discovery of the foundation of the Baths of Trajan.

Top: The Basilica of Constantine.

by a statue of St. Peter at the end of the 16th century.
Rubble had accumulated near the column, and it was
surrounded by more recent buildings.

The Excavation of 1810

Pius VI had had its base cleared down to the ancient
paving stones so that it stood in a kind of ditch, bordered
to the south by the convents of St. Euphemia and the
Holy Ghost, to the west by a number of buildings, and
to the north by two churches. The plan of 1810 was
to widen the square and, by digging it up, bring the
ground to a uniform level, and then to excavate it. The
demolition of the buildings and of the two convents
was begun in March 1812 and completed in December
of that year. Excavations began the following May.

The first results were not very encouraging: a few
broken columns, a vase, a head. A year later, the finds
included various statues, an empress' head, and a
fragment of a colossal statue made of porphyry, a dark-
red or purple stone.

The most important building to be uncovered was the
central section of the ancient Basilica Ulpia, but several
pieces of the portico of the libraries were found as well.
Bases of twenty columns and the remains of marble
flagstones of the basilica were revealed. The space cleared
in this way was a vast shallow pit surrounded by a wall.

Work continued on the square through the 19th and
into the first years of the 20th century. It was followed
by large-scale clearing projects organized by Benito
Mussolini in the 1930s.

The "Garden of the Capitol," an Unwieldy Project

Near Trajan's Forum, the most ancient district of
Rome was desolate and dilapidated. The arena of the
Colosseum was completely covered with soil and
rubble; part of the facade had collapsed, and another
part was held up by a kind of spur that had been built
in 1803. The work done under Pius VII had not really
changed the appearance of the Forum. And as for the
two temples near the Tiber, they appeared to be sinking
into the ground.

In order to provide a fitting setting for this group of

Napoleon had the
Vendôme Column
(above) erected in Paris,
modeling it on Trajan's
Column (opposite).

After the Napoleonic
excavations in 1820
Pope Pius VII had
Trajan's Forum
surrounded by a wall
(opposite below).

Right: The Temple of Antoninus and Faustina was built in AD 141 by Antoninus Pius in honor of his wife, Faustina; it was dedicated to the emperor on his death in 161. The temple is one of the best-preserved monuments of Rome and of the Forum.

Left above: The Temple of Concord.

Left below: Giuseppe Valadier, an architect who assisted with the excavation of Trajan's Forum and other projects.

monuments, plans were made to create a huge archaeological promenade, the "Garden of the Capitol." It was supposed to include the Capitol, the Forum, and the Colosseum. This project, which eventually proved to be too costly and unwieldy and was never completed, involved the demolition of the modern buildings (which, needless to say, would have aroused the hostility of the inhabitants), the uncovering of the monuments, and, most important, the leveling of the ground over a vast area. In spite of these obstacles work began in 1810: Six hundred workers were employed in the Forum.

The Work Got Under Way

They began by uncovering the Temple of Concord, the Temple of Antoninus and Faustina, and the Basilica of Constantine, the floor of which was covered with so much earth that the vaults barely appeared above the ground. A year later the three naves had been cleared down to the flagstones. Near the Arch of Titus, the convent of Santa Francesca Romana, which abutted the arch, was demolished, as was the church that had been built over the ruins of the Temple of Venus and Rome.

A young French architect, J.-F. Ménager, led an excavation of the Temple of Antoninus and Faustina. He uncovered the bases of the columns and the stairs up to the building and drew an idealized reconstruction of it (below).

The bases of both of the ancient buildings were uncovered in the last stage of the project.

Architects Assisting Archaeology

Architects participated actively in the archaeological work and decisively altered the conception of what an

Ménager's drawing includes many errors; the portrayal of the apotheosis of Antoninus and Faustina on the pediment, for example, is completely imaginary. Above: A detail showing a capital.

excavation really entailed. They demanded the comprehensive clearing of the lower layers of a building and put the emphasis on architectural groups that enabled the complete topography of a site to be reconstructed. This was the approach followed by Carlo Fea, who attempted to rediscover the structure of the Forum and planned a vast excavation of Ostia, Rome's ancient port to the west on the Tiber.

Such, also, was the vision of Giuseppi Guattani, a member of the Commission for the Embellishment of Rome and an associate on the project of the restoration of the Forum. In his *Guide to Rome,* he advised visitors to climb to the top of Trajan's Column to understand the layout of the city. He suggested the use of a schematic map of the monuments so that the dynamics of their interrelationships could be grasped. The guides produced in the 19th century were no longer merely descriptions of the city; recent topographical analyses and assessments of the archaeological discoveries had shed light on the structural organization of the sites, and thereby all of Rome.

A Time of Assessments

The projects of this period were undoubtedly overly ambitious. The French occupation, which was at first, in the words of the French writer François-Auguste-René de Chateaubriand, "despicable and despoiling," and later merely "iniquitous," aroused an almost universal

In addition to the projects he organized to restore the ancient monuments, Napoleon wanted to enlarge the square in front of the Pantheon and open a promenade to the north of Rome. Most of his projects remained on the drawing board, but the area of the Piazza del Popolo, notably the Pincio (left), was transformed in accordance with the terms of Article 7 of Napoleon's decree of 27 July 1811: "The plans that have been submitted to us for the promenade near the Square of the People are hereby approved. To this effect, the convent of the People and its dependencies shall be demolished; this promenade shall be called the Garden of the Great Caesar."

hostility—and yet archaeology benefited from it enormously. The French novelist Stendhal, whose critical mind was always ready to become inflamed, could testify to that: "Thanks to the immense projects that have been undertaken, the appearance of the ancient monuments has changed completely since 1809, and the scholarship that concerns itself with them has become more reasonable."

Major scholarly excavations took place in the Forum, on the Appian Way, and in the catacombs during the 19th century. This was also a time of classification and ordering of materials—texts, inscriptions, and objects—that had been accumulated since the Renaissance in a sometimes disordered and hasty manner.

CHAPTER V
THE AGE OF REASON

In May 1864 crowds assembled at the Palace of Cardinal Righetti, located over the ruins of Pompey's Theater, in order to witness the raising of a gilded bronze Hercules nearly thirteen feet tall (opposite).

The equestrian statue of Marcus Aurelius (right).

In 1863, nearing the 2600th anniversary of the founding of Rome, an item of news was stirring scholarly circles: An exceptionally important statue had just been discovered at the Prima Porta, one of the city gates. Scholars had known for a long time that Livia Drusilla, the wife of Emperor Augustus, had had a magnificent villa built for herself to the north of Rome.

An amateur named Giuseppe Gagliardi had identified the site. On 20 April, below ground level, near a large room decorated with blue and green landscapes, he discovered a statue of Augustus in perfect condition. Pope Pius IX immediately claimed the masterpiece: It would fit so well in the Chiaramonti Museum!

The Good Fortune of Amateur Archaeologists

Amateurs such as Gagliardi had no difficulty obtaining permission from the Holy See to open their own excavations in exchange for a share of the discoveries. It was an amateur who found the paving stones of the ancient Via Latina to the south of Rome, and on each side of it, a number of tombs that were rich in paintings, stuccos, and funerary objects, some of which were sold and dispersed. And another discovered one of the great stores of marble of antiquity: a large number of blocks of alabaster, onyx, and serpentine in the antique colors of yellow, green, and red from 2nd-century BC Emporium, one of the ancient ports of Rome. Pius IX distributed these materials to churches all over the world and showered the lucky explorer with his favors, including making him a baron.

Later, the history of archaeology still included such chance discoveries—sensational news that attracted illustrious visitors as well as pillaging and scandal. In the 1860s everyone heard about the trial of the Marchese Giovanni Campana, a

In the *Augustus of Primaporta,* the emperor projects a serene majesty. The universe is engraved upon his breastplate: A bearded old man at the top represents the sky; to the left is the Chariot of the Sun, accompanied by the winged Dawn and the spirit of Sunrise; on the lower part are the Earth, Apollo, and Artemis.

collector who was banished from Rome for extorting considerable sums of money from pawnbrokers.

But this was also a time of major and systematic excavations led by such archaeologists as Antonio Nibby, whose research was objective and whose method was the most scientific.

Nibby, Fea: Quarrels in the Forum

In 1827 Antonio Nibby was appointed director of the excavations in the Forum. He cleared the northern part of it, the Tabularium, the Temple of Concord, and the Temple of Venus and Rome. In the course of his work, however, he arrived at conclusions that put him at loggerheads

with Carlo Fea, the former commissioner of antiquities, and most other archaeologists.

At the foot of the Capitoline Hill near the Temple of Saturn stood three columns. Their entablature bore a fragment of an inscription—ESTITVER—that led scholars to believe the columns to be the remains of the

Fenced off, full of trees and birds, the garden in the fresco in the House of Livia (top) has a charm and an air of mystery that are unique in Roman painting.

The Tomb of Pomponius Hylas was discovered in 1831. The main hall of the columbarium (above) is decorated with stuccos and paintings.

DU·TEMPLE·
DE·LA·PAIX

Temple of Jupiter Tonans (the Thunderer). Nibby relied
on recent discoveries and old texts to restore the true
interpretation: In the *Einsiedeln Itinerary*, the medieval
guide to Rome, he found the entire inscription, proving
that in fact these columns were the remains of the
Temple of Vespasian. This temple was built in honor
of the emperor, who ruled from AD 69 to 79, and
was completed on the death of his son, Titus. The
emperors Caracalla and Antonius had it restored—
[R]ESTITVER[VNT]—two centuries later.

In the same way, the archaeologist identified
the three brick vaults that stand on the left of
the Forum as one looks toward the Colosseum. In the
Middle Ages this huge building was thought to be the
Temple of Romulus. It had been referred to as the
Temple of Peace since the 15th century. But in Nibby's
view it could only be the Basilica of Constantine, which
had been built at the beginning of the 4th century.

At the same time, in spite of Fea's protests, Nibby
identified the true Temple of Peace, an impressive
architectural group where the emperor Vespasian had
assembled "all that men were curious about"—gold vases
from Judea, statues, and a rich library. The famous

Stendhal liked to
poke fun at Antonio
Nibby (above), who
changed the names of
the monuments. And
yet, without even
crediting him, Stendahl
"borrowed" whole
pages of Nibby's
Roman Itinerary in his
own writing.

Forma Urbis was sealed there in the 3rd century AD.

Discourse on Method

These scholarly disputes did not escape the irony of the satirists, who also lampooned the extreme conservatism of the antiquarians.

Yet methods of analysis had progressed. In the 16th century dogmatism and falsification had been the standard weapons of scholars who, like artists, sought a model in Rome: "What I established on the Forum," declared Bartolomeo Marliano, "is the absolute truth; and if old Romulus himself had risen from his tomb to tell me that he had built his forum differently, I would answer him thus: 'Oh Romulus! You have crossed the River Lethe, and because of that you have forgotten the location of your city to such an extent that you do not know what you are saying!'" The 19th century saw the triumph of the philological spirit. The critical method applied to texts was also applied to the works of art and monuments, which scholars attempted to identify, date, and locate.

Historical analysis of the findings was not attempted until the end of the 19th century. By about 1850 the excavation of the Forum had almost been completed. Its structure was now better understood, thanks to Nibby's

Opposite: This 1814 drawing of the "Temple of Peace," the Basilica of Constantine, presents an architectural reconstruction of the lateral part of the temple.

The drawings on this page depict the Napoleonic excavations of the Forum.

Overleaf: An 1815 print showing the remains of ancient Rome.

106

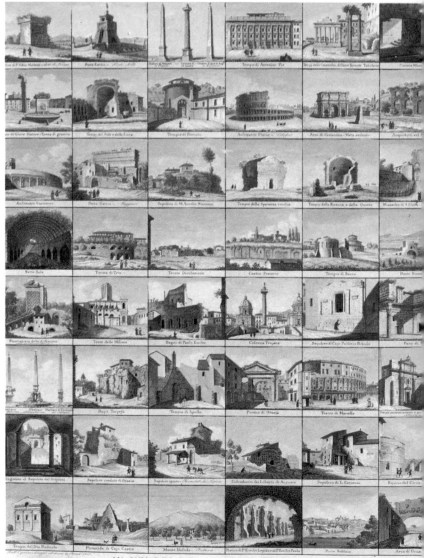

AVANZI DEI PIU COSPICUI EDIFICJ ANTICHI DI ROMA
Alla Nobile Donzella la Sig.ra Marchesa

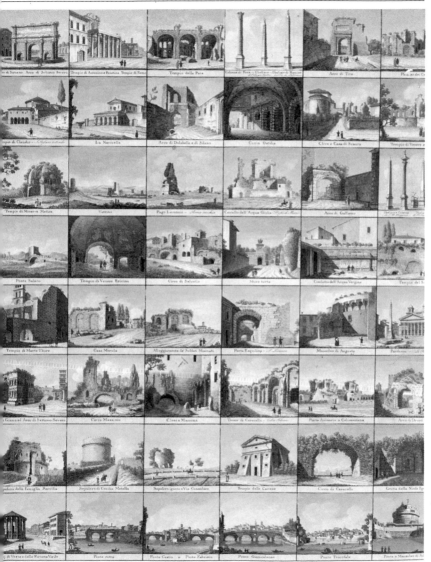

IACENZE COME SI OSSERVANO NELL'ANNO MDCCCXV

Giulia Zondadari gia Chigi di Siena

reconstructions and the work of Theodor Mommsen (1817–1903) in 1845. This German scholar had determined the location of the *comitium,* the place where ancient Romans had held assemblies. After 1850 other excavations were begun: Some were on the Palatine Hill, where the House of Livia—a part of the Temple of Apollo (thought at the time to be the Temple of the Victorious Jupiter)—and the remains of the imperial palaces were uncovered. On the Appian Way fresh excavations were entrusted to Luigi Canina.

The Tomb of Caecilia Metella was built in the late 1st century BC. Its drum shape, like that of the Tomb of Augustus, attests to the influence of the Orient and Greece on Roman funerary architecture.

The Queen of Roads

Begun in the 4th century by Appius Claudius, who gave it his name, the more than 350-mile-long Appian Way eventually crossed the Roman peninsula from Rome to Brindisi. Lined with cypresses, pines, and olive trees, it led to various temples, villas, and funerary structures. (According to an old tradition, the ancients buried their dead outside the city, in places through which people traveled; the Romans, it was said, wished to show those

This tomb on the Appian Way is among the most frequently drawn monuments. For a long time it was called Capo di Bove, "the Bull's Head," because of the bull's heads that adorn its frieze, a traditional decoration on funerary monuments.

who passed by that they, too, were mortals.) Five miles outside of Rome the road divided at the place where the legendary Horatii were said to have fought the Curiatii. Their tombs, in the form of mounds, lay a little beyond, on the right side of the road.

In the Middle Ages nobles occupied and fortified some of the structures along the Appian Way, including the Tomb of Caecilia Metella, a mausoleum shaped like a tower that served as a keep for a massive fortified castle. Other remains were used as sources of building materials. Still others were simply abandoned, becoming hideouts for bandits. Renaissance artists—including Raphael and Michelangelo—appealed in vain for the Appian Way to be saved. By the 19th century, its outline was disappearing amid the ruined tombs.

P aved with slabs of basalt and bordered by sidewalks of beaten earth, the Appian Way, stretching from Rome to the opposite side of the peninsula, was wide enough (about thirteen feet) to allow vehicles to pass in both directions. Every seven or ten miles, travelers found relay posts, for changing horses, and an inn.

B elow: A tomb on the Appian Way.

Luigi Canina, the Restorer of the Appian Way

The 1850 plan had several aims: to restore the whole extent of the road, to reveal its line, and to uncover what was left of it. Three years of intensive work were devoted to the road's first section. Canina wrote very detailed commentaries and recorded the state of the road and its restoration in large engraved plates. He imagined the long series of tombs that stood on the site, some of them monumental and decorated with stucco and frescoes, others simple altars. In this way he described almost three thousand tombs along the first nine or ten miles of the road: pyramid-shaped ones, round drumlike ones, or formal ones resembling temples. Doubts have been cast on Canina's reconstructions as a result of excavations made in our own century, but his plates give us an excellent idea of what those great consular roads must once have looked like leaving the gates of the capital and crossing the empire. Their common symbolic starting point was marked by the golden column that Augustus had placed in the center of the Forum.

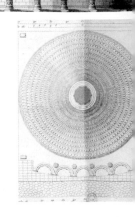

The Revival of Christian Archaeology

The Greek and Roman gods and heroes of the ancient republic were no longer the only idols of the 19th

RELIQVIE DEL GRANDE MONVMENTO DENOMINATO CASAL ROTONDO

The Appian Way was in use for several centuries: It was flanked by tombs whose variety of periods and forms explains the attraction the queen of roads had for travelers: shelters in the form of temples, simple altars, tombs with podiums, exedrae (large semicircular seating areas), and drumlike forms such as the Casal Rotondo (left), a tomb 115 feet in diameter.

ESPOSIZIONE DELL'INTERA ARCHITETTVRA DEL GRANDE MONVMENTO
DI MESSALA CORVINO VLTIMATO DA M.VALERIO MESSALINO COTTA

century. The field of archaeological exploration was now extended to the whole of the Mediterranean and to the Middle East. Such figures as German scholar Heinrich Schliemann, the discoverer of Troy, French archaeologist Jacques-Joseph Champollion and his brother Jean-François Champollion, an Egyptologist, came to the fore. The Etruscan and Mesopotamian civilizations were unearthed. In Rome new territory—the catacombs—was rediscovered.

The catacomb of St. Sebastian was one of the few that were known about at the beginning of the 19th century; since Bosio's time, most of these underground cemeteries had largely been abandoned or even forgotten. A scholar, Giuseppe Marchi, was the first to draw Pope Gregory XVI's attention to the need to safeguard this evidence of Christian history. In 1841 Marchi was entrusted with their supervision, and in 1854 he was put in charge of the founding of the Christian Museum of the Lateran. Giovanni Battista de' Rossi, a disciple of Marchi's, decided to make a precise map of the catacombs at the same time.

He consulted a wide variety of traditional literary and ecclesiastical sources and medieval documents: itineraries, catalogues of relics, and catalogues of cemeteries. By cross-checking all of these documents, De' Rossi claimed to be able to determine the location of the crypt of St. Sixtus, and, in

The catacombs are underground cemeteries where sanctuaries were later built near the tombs of the martyrs. On these two pages are engravings of the catacombs from De' Rossi's *Underground Christian Rome*.

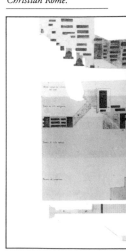

that very location, he found the inscription NELIVS MARTYR. He knew from the texts that Pope Cornelius had been buried in AD 253 close to Sixtus' grave.

Prolonged excavation enabled him to find the crypt, as well as the whole of the Catacomb of St. Callistus. De' Rossi then realized why the crypt had remained buried for so long: Following many invasions, during which the tombs of the martyrs had been ransacked, in the 4th century AD Pope Damasus I and his successors had had wide staircases built in the underground galleries, wide enough for the pilgrims to descend directly to the sites they wanted to visit. Passages were cut into the sanctuaries to allow air and light to enter. With time, these structures collapsed, blocking the galleries and tunnels. Until De' Rossi's time, the archaeologists had stopped at these heaps of earth, but he dug through them, passed on, and discovered the heart of the catacombs.

Cross sections of the catacombs (below).

Giovanni Battista de' Rossi, the Undisputed Prince of Underground Rome

By following the same method, De' Rossi uncovered twenty-six catacombs, opening galleries that had lain

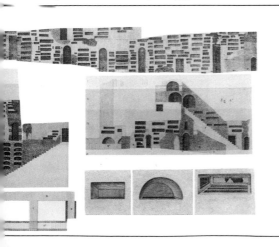

buried for nearly ten centuries. In the underground basilicas ceremonies were again conducted, and pilgrims came. Representations of the tombs and their frescoes spread throughout the world. Sacred art once again became a subject of study and admiration. Pope Pius IX himself came to visit these famous places.

The religious fervor aroused by these discoveries, as well as the influence of the church, especially the Jesuits, might have become an obstacle to the advance of Christian archaeology, but De' Rossi was able to convince scholars of his findings. He was invited to collaborate with Mommsen and another German scholar on the publication of the great corpus of Latin inscriptions. For thirteen years, 1864 to 1877, he worked on his book, *Underground Christian Rome,* in which he examined the funerary practices of the first Christians, the very abundant graffiti found on the walls, and a few of the most famous catacombs, including copies of their frescoes and inscriptions. Starting in 1863 De' Rossi edited the *Bulletin of Christian Archaeology.* By the end of his life he had published more than two hundred texts. After his death new discoveries continued to be made. There are now sixty-seven known catacombs in Rome.

The Demanding and Difficult Work of the Archaeologist: to Excavate, Interpret, Classify, and Inform

Pope Pius IX visits the "crypt of the popes."

All the scholars of the period were busy classifying and defining their discipline, and those working on antiquity benefited from this great wave of rational thought. New methods of establishing correct editions of texts were

devised; catalogues raisonnés of objects were published, as were the great collections of Greek and Latin inscriptions, which were presented in topographical order. The museums also prepared thematic catalogues of their collections. The dissemination of information improved. Various publications presented accounts of

Overleaf: American tourists visit the catacombs and discover a skeleton in underground Rome in 1900.

recent discoveries and commented on them, while new associations financed further exploration. The Roman Academy, founded in 1810, brought together archaeologists and amateurs, artists and clerics who aspired to be the heirs of Pomponius Laetus and the humanists. They organized lavish banquets and visited the ruins together.

The Founding of the Great Archaeological Institutes

The Institute of Archaeological Correspondence was created in 1829, at the initiative of archaeologists and artists, and with the support of kings Ludwig I of Bavaria and Frederick III of Prussia. The institute published a bulletin and annals that described discoveries made all over the world. For nearly forty years, the history of archaeology was linked to that institute; its international role dwindled only as a result of the Franco-Prussian War of 1870. From then on it was controlled solely by the Germans and became the German Archaeological Institute. Its activities extended to Athens, Cairo, and Istanbul. In 1873 the French founded another institution, the French School of Rome.

Sculptural fragments from the Palatine in an 1870 photograph by John Henry Parker (left).

Entrance to the Catacomb of St. Domitilla (opposite).

The engraving below was printed on the frontispiece of the second volume of *Unpublished Monuments,* an official publication of the German Archaeological Institute. The temple of archaeological science rises amid the Forum and the Palatine; its steps lead to the library inside. On the pediment, we see a representation of Rome, flanked by the Tiber and Tarpeia; between its columns, the heads of the *Dioscuri,* much admired by Neo-Classicists.

By this time the progress made in archaeology could no longer be questioned. Even if the explorers were sometimes amateurs, and even though the antiquarian spirit persisted, there were now also genuine scholars at work on genuine excavation projects.

Archaeology, however, needed to develop new methods, in-depth excavations, and a historical approach. Shortly before his death, in his book *Rome in the Year 1838,* Nibby wrote: "Nothing remains on the surface of the ground. But I, who was born amid these ruins and who have lived in them, I can testify that in all the cellars of all the houses of this region, and in many of the walls, there is evidence to prove that if one were to excavate the ground and demolish the houses, one would find exceptionally important information concerning the ancient topography of Rome and the history of the arts."

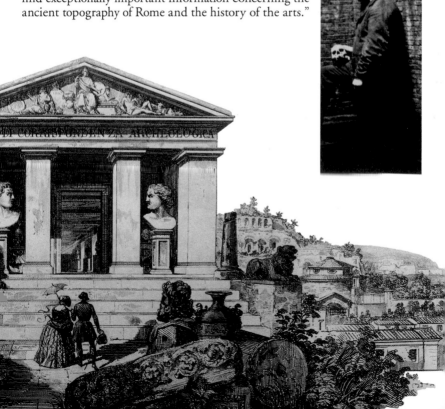

In the 20th century archaeology entered the modern era and found its methodology. After centuries of isolated excavations and discoveries limited to the republican and imperial periods, the earlier Rome—the Rome of the kings—arose from the depths of the earth, gradually revealing the mysterious origins of the city.

CHAPTER VI
FROM ONE MYTH TO ANOTHER

The discovery of the *Seated Gladiator* (opposite), 1885.

"I have never experienced an impression as extraordinary as when I saw that almost barbarian athlete who seemed to be awakening from a thousand-year-long sleep after long and terrible struggles."
Rodolfo Lanciani

In the wake of Italian unification, major work began on the Esquiline, one of Rome's seven hills, to create a new district; at this time many remains of the houses, villas, and tombs were discovered. In this 1871 photograph, which shows a site being excavated near a building called the Temple of Minerva Medica, the workers have revealed part of an ancient brick wall.

In 1861 Italy began the process of national unification, and in 1870 Rome was declared the capital of the new country. The new monarchy wanted a capital city that was worthy of the ancient city and the city of the popes. In this "third Rome," everything still had to be built:

Below: Objects found during the construction of the new city, photographed in 1874.

Neither the populace nor the new administration could move into the palaces or the hovels. An unimagined Rome appeared beneath the spade and the pickax, but many remains disappeared beneath modern buildings. Some old districts—a large part of the medieval city, including several monasteries and many palaces and famous villas—were wiped from the map.

"They are building furiously," wrote the indignant German historian Ferdinand Gregorovius, "the districts and the hills are being turned upside down.... Every hour, I see a piece of ancient Rome falling.... The old city is disappearing...." All that archaeologist Rodolfo

Lanciani wrote in reply, in defense of the construction projects, was a list of the discoveries made between 1870 and 1885: "705 amphorae, 2360 lamps, 1824 inscriptions, 77 columns of pink marble, 313 pieces of columns, 157 capitals, 18 sarcophagi, 36,679 gold, silver, and bronze coins."

In fact, since the late 16th century under Sixtus V's rule, never had so much been destroyed or discovered without the slightest thought being given to urban design. On the Esquiline, Quirinal, and Viminal hills, Roman houses containing frescoes, mosaics, and sculptures—even a whole necropolis—came to light. Bas-reliefs, terra-cottas, domestic objects, and statues, including a bronze Bacchus with long hair, an armless Apollo, and a life-size head of Aphrodite, were recovered from the Tiber. When the banks of the river were worked on, the gardens of the Villa Farnesina were excavated, revealing one of the finest series of frescoes and stuccos found up to that time. What emotion there must have been in seeing the myth of Phaëthon, the legend of Dionysus, and genre paintings glorifying love all emerging from the depths of the

Above: A fresco found near the Farnesina.

These examples of the ancient art of stucco (below) from the villa found beneath the Farnesina were among the most famous.

earth. Everything about these remains was extremely fine, especially the stuccos, where the details of every gesture, every piece of clothing, seemed to be the trace of a fossil.

Italian Archaeology Reaches Maturity

These discoveries, the history of which is very similar to those of previous centuries, enriched the National Museum of Rome, which was installed in 1889 in the Baths of Diocletian. Italy's King Victor Emmanuel II was genuinely preoccupied with protecting the artistic heritage of his country. In 1870 he founded the administration of the excavations and the conservation of the monuments of the province of Rome. In 1875 he created the Italian School of Archaeology. It was modeled on the French and German institutes and encouraged

the resumption of the excavations in the "monumental center" of Rome. On the Palatine, what was known as Domitian's Stadium was uncovered; in the Colosseum, the whole of the underground passages and chambers was revealed. In the Forum, first the central area was cleared, and then the ground of the entire site was leveled. "From February to April 1882," wrote Lanciani, "more than 10,200 cubic meters of earth were removed and cleared, and 2800 square meters of ancient ground were uncovered. Twenty-six inscriptions and a large number of remains of monuments were found.... For the first time since the fall of the Roman Empire, one could walk along the entire length of the Via Sacra from where it started to the Capitoline."

Had the Ancients Told the Truth?

In June 1899, in the northwestern part of the Forum, Giacomo Boni uncovered a slab of black marble

Though trained as an architect, Giacomo Boni (1859–1925, left) was especially interested in geology and construction techniques. Before him, archaeologists were topographers and scholars whose excavations were guided by texts and who delegated fieldwork. Boni took up the spade and pickax himself and thus became a pioneer of active archaeology. In contrast to his peers, he believed archaeology served to reconstruct the history of a site from its origins, a goal that could be attained only by stratigraphy—uncovering the different layers systematically. Boni's contemporaries retained almost nothing of his lessons. The stratigraphic method was not applied systematically to Classical sites until the 1960s.

In 1875 excavations made around the Colosseum revealed underground service passages that were used during the games. In ancient times they were covered by an enormous wooden platform. Here, the inside of the Colosseum before and after the excavations.

that was almost square (about ten by thirteen feet), surrounded by a white line. The ancient authors spoke of the existence of a black stone in the Forum, the *lapis niger*. According to some, it marked the location of Romulus' tomb; others said that it was the tomb of Faustulus, Romulus' foster father, and still others the tomb of Hostilian, the third king of Rome.

Hoping to reach this mysterious tomb, Boni dug deeper: Under the marble appeared an archaic grouping made up of what seemed to be a kind of tomb (it was, in fact, an altar) and a stela that was covered with inscriptions. The text, which is written partly in boustrophedon (a system of writing from left to right and then right to left, and so on), is still difficult to comprehend: The letters are too close to each other, and it is barely possible to make out a few words. Only the first sentence has been completely deciphered: "Whoever violates this sacred place shall be destined for the infernal gods." The appearance of this prohibition,

In August 1899 it was decided to clear the whole of the space that stretched from the Temple of Antoninus and Faustina (above center in the photograph) to the Curia. An enormous amount of earth was removed, and a large number of houses were demolished. The Basilica Aemilia, a building dating from the republican period, was revealed.

Above: Guido Baccelli, a government minister, visits the excavations.

undoubtedly a sacred archaic law from the 6th century BC, associated with sanctuaries dedicated to Vulcan, the Roman god of fire, unleashed a historical debate.

Germans Against Italians: Patriotic Archaeology

For several years, German historians had questioned the value of the ancient texts, especially those of Livy, concerning the origins of the city. Opposing this so-called hypercritical school were most of the Italians, who were "traditionalists." They believed in the texts.

The black stone appeared to prove the Italians right: Did it not confirm the traditional story of the founding of Rome? Debate was acrimonious and had an effect on public opinion, further dividing the Italians from the Germans.

The controversy was revived in 1902 and again in 1907, with the successive discoveries of two necropoli from the 9th and 8th centuries BC near the Temple of Antoninus and Faustina and on the Quirinal. At the same time, Boni was uncovering the bases of huts dating from the same period on the Palatine. Now the debate did not last long, however, even though the new revelations corroborated the statements of the ancients on the settlements of the hills in very early times. Because their training was inadequate and their methods insufficient, the archaeologists were not ready to undertake difficult excavations. Boni himself preferred not to take his investigations any further, even though he was the only archaeologist who would have been able to do so, since he was the first one to apply the stratigraphic method to historical excavation.

The discovery of the *lapis niger* near the Arch of Septimius Severus attracted crowds. Here Baccelli is depicted inspecting the dig.

A 20th-Century Antiquarian: Rodolfo Lanciani

At this time, archaeologists still largely devoted their time to topography. Lanciani studied the Forma Urbis, the marble map from the 3rd century. He drew up a new archaeological map of the city using a scale of one to one thousand and produced extremely erudite plates that detailed the chronology of the discoveries made since the 15th century. Lanciani belonged to the old antiquarian school, which was less concerned with analysis than with description and assembly; for this map he used his own remarkable knowledge of the city. Lanciani liked to explore the least-known parts of the Roman countryside, as people had in the 16th century. One can tell that he really saw Rome stone by stone. Indeed, he inspected all the excavation sites at a time when the city was being cut up and moved in every direction, once again giving up its soul.

By this point it was photographs rather than drawings that archaeologists were bringing back with them from their lengthy investigations. At the time they barely understood the importance of photography, which Boni had used in the Forum, shooting from an aerostatic balloon. The English archaeologist John Henry Parker had been the first to employ this new method for scholarly purposes in 1870.

The Cult of *Romanità*

In 1911 Lanciani organized a great exhibition to celebrate the fiftieth anniversary of Italian unity. Here the most important archaeological discoveries were put on show—with pride of place going to the Augustus statue from the Prima Porta. On the eve of the Libyan expedition of the Turkish-Italian War, the monarchy considered it important to demonstrate that Roman civilization was still thriving, as shown by the roads, bridges, and monuments that were always portrayed within the landscape of the ancient provinces. The myth of Rome, which had served political ambitions since the Middle Ages, thus survived in modern Italy. Italian unity and Roman identity were celebrated together.

Fascism gave this idea its most extreme expression.

Born in London in 1806, John Henry Parker (below) was a scholar fascinated by the history of architecture. In 1866 he decided to photograph all the major ancient monuments systematically.

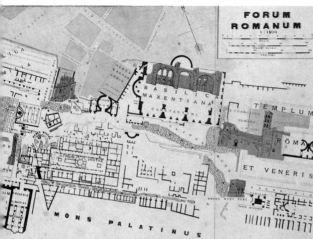

The major work of Rodolfo Lanciani (1845–1929), *The Forma Urbis,* shows Rome as it appeared in three eras: antiquity, the Middle Ages, and the late 19th century. His plan of the Forum is still quite accurate, apart from a few details, in spite of recent discoveries that have revealed a number of early remains between the Atrium Vestae and the Arch of Titus.

Left: Parker's photograph of the Arch of Titus.

"Five years from now," Mussolini declared on 31 December 1925, "Rome must appear in all its splendor: immense, ordered, and as powerful as it was at the time of the first empire, that of Augustus." The impetus given to Classical studies and to Roman history, the eagle that symbolized the regime, and the insistence on reviving Latin as a "speakable language" all focused on the exaltation of Roman identity. It was hardly surprising that the Fascists wanted archaeology to play an essential role in their propaganda. Giglioli, the archaeologist of Mussolini's regime, evoked "the development of archaeological research in relation to the historical and national aims of Fascism." He gave historians the task of demonstrating the continuity of the history of Rome, the permanence of the Roman nation,

"One order from Benito Mussolini, and everything that is considered unworthy disappears from the map," commented a journal of the period.

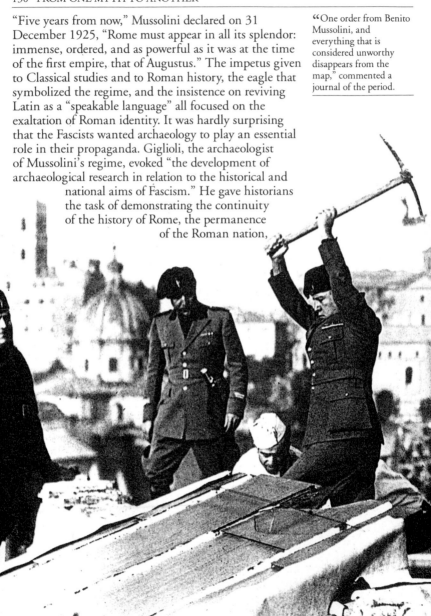

and the grandeur it had enjoyed since its origin.

With the collaboration of a large number of archaeologists, Mussolini planned a vast program of excavations. In the mass of projects, two groups illustrate in the clearest possible way the political use of history, a concept he was fond of. On the one hand, there was the restoration of the Augustan city, and on the other, the excavation of the imperial forums and of Ostia, which was linked to the construction of the Via del Mare, the road to the sea. This road was the symbol and axis of the extension of Rome toward the Mediterranean. As in previous centuries, the archaeological programs were indistinguishable from the renovation of the city.

Mussolini ordered both destruction and construction. Once again, the small squares and narrow streets of Rome were dug up to bring to the surface "that civilization that is buried but not dead."

Mussolini did, of course, have ulterior motives in invoking Augustus. The new regime posed as the champion of harmony, peace, and a return to order. Above: A statue of Mussolini as Augustus.

The pickax in this photograph symbolizes perfectly the way the Fascists massacred the city. Here, Mussolini himself wields the ax to open the excavation of the Via Dell'Impero.

The Ara Pacis (opposite and below) consisted of an enclosed podium reached via a staircase. The altar is inside the enclosure. Important members of the imperial family are depicted on the southern frieze, a detail of which is shown at left. Agrippa, Augustus' son-in-law, is the figure to the right.

The 2000th Anniversary of Augustus: Fascist Rome Celebrates Imperial Rome

After the clearing of the Forum of Augustus, which was done casually, without any measurement or inventory, the celebration of Augustus culminated in 1937–8, on the 2000th anniversary of his

birth. His mausoleum was cleared, restored, and isolated by the creation of the Piazza Augusto Imperatore; the Altar of Peace, the Ara Pacis, was completely restored and replaced nearby, close to the river. Last and most important of all, in 1937 there was an extremely spectacular exhibition, the "Mostra Augustea della Romanità."

The organizers of 1937 were much more ambitious than Rodolfo Lanciani had been in 1911: They wanted this to be the greatest exhibition of the century. They commissioned maps, drawings, photographs, plaster casts, and, most important, more than three hundred models of famous monuments from all over the empire. These were placed in a special room, in which a relief map of Rome celebrated the magnificence of the

Erected in 9 BC, the Ara Pacis was one of the most important symbols of Augustan imperial propaganda, exalting Rome's universal dominion and divine origin. Various fragments of the structure had been found in the 16th and 19th centuries but it was not until 1937–8 that it was fully excavated. On the occasion of Augustus' 2000th anniversary, the altar was set up near Augustus' mausoleum beside the Tiber and protected by a structure of glass and concrete. The terms of the emperor's will were inscribed on the walls of the monument. It was dedicated on 23 September 1938.

Greatness Rediscovered

On 23 September 1937 the "Mostra Augustea della Romanità" opened in the Palace of Expositions on the Via Nazionale, featuring a display of photographs and scale models of amphitheaters, bridges, and baths. A plan of the city was designed based on Lanciani's *The Forma Urbis*. The materials from the exposition were to have been reused for the Universal Exposition of Rome in 1942, which was supposed to celebrate the conquest of Ethiopia and the twentieth anniversary of the regime. A whole district in southern Rome was set aside for the exposition, but work was interrupted by World War II and the defeat of Fascism and was not completed until the 1950s. The Museum of Roman Civilization was opened in 1955; today it houses the materials from the 1911 and 1937 expositions.

Left: A reconstruction of the Colosseum.

Pages 136–7: A model of ancient Rome.

Pages 138–9: A watercolor reconstruction of the Roman Forum.

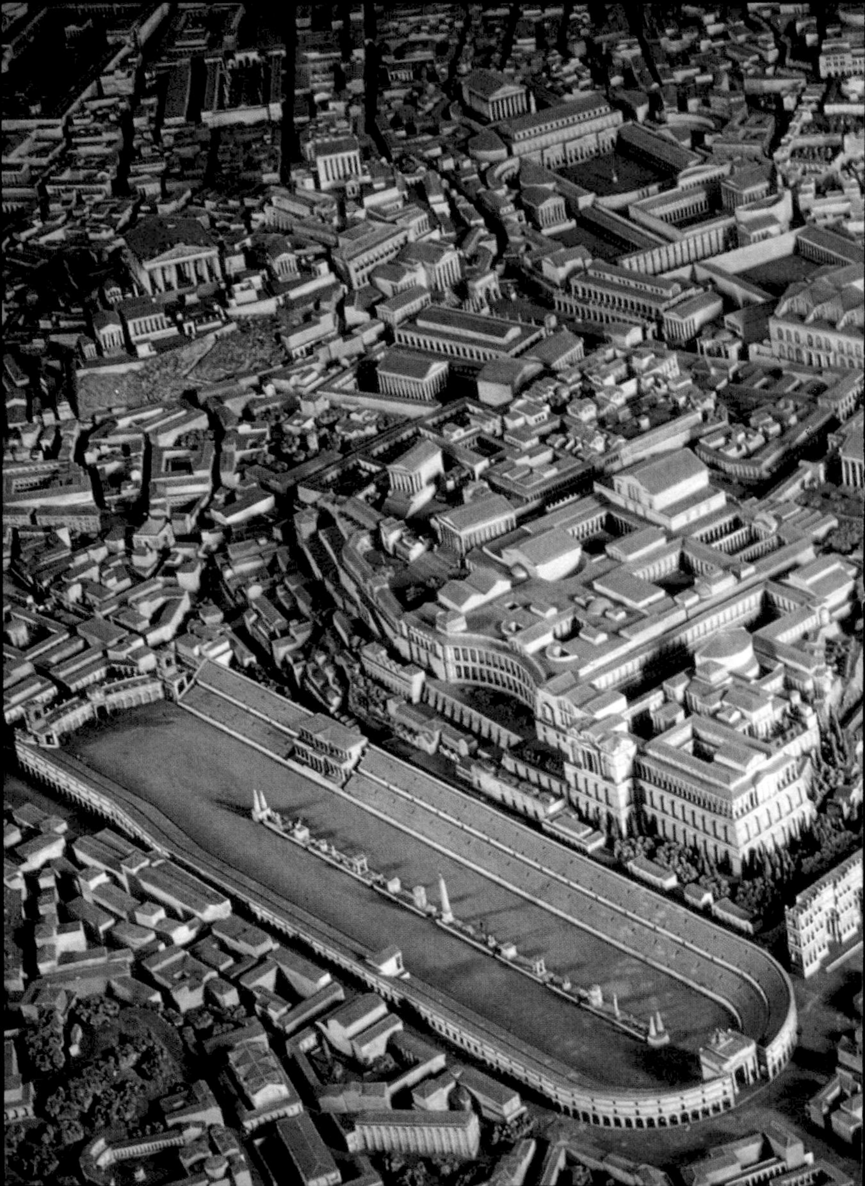

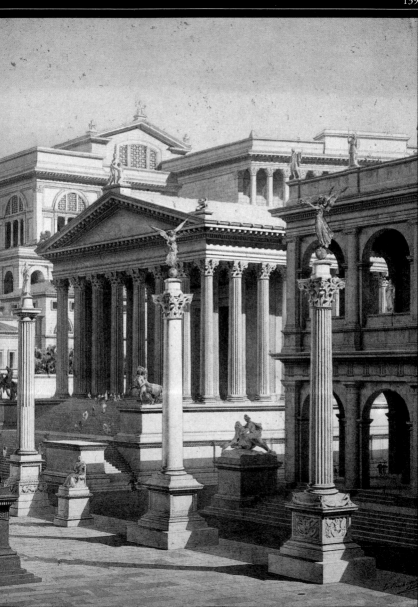

city at the beginning of the 4th century. Many other
countries contributed to this exhibition as well, creating a
sense of solidarity with Mussolini.

In addition, the exhibition was a scholarly success.
It was the first-ever assemblage of the documents
and evidence in every shape and form that had
been scattered all over the world. However, in his
opening speech, Giglioli did not hide the political
role of the enterprise: *Romanità* was
proclaimed the mother of all, and
Mussolini was acclaimed as its defender,
the guarantor of glories to come.

Mussolini, of course, was not satisfied with
such gestures. He demanded a grander stroke:
He wanted to give Rome its opening onto
the sea at Ostia. To link the city with
the coast he needed a glorious road,
along which the imperial forums
would be restored. Five maps were

The Theater of Ostia
(with a capacity of
three thousand) was
restored in the 1930s. At
the back of the orchestra
and the semicircular
stage, on the site of the
former arched portico,
marble architectural
pieces have been
installed, including these
three masks.

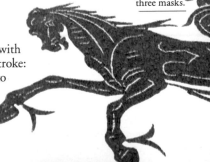

put on display showing the Roman conquests from the beginning up to the Fascist empire.

An Assessment of Fascist Archaeology

Mussolini also had the site of Ostia excavated. The ancient port of Rome had already been explored in the 18th century. Carlo Fea had sent fifty prisoners there to carry out some large-scale clearing projects, but he soon had to give that up, as the region was too marshy.

Work had begun again later, for a longer period of time, under Pius IX, revealing statues and important pictorial series. In 1910 the archaeologist Vaglieri discovered a winged statue of Minerva Victrix there; the fact that she was "victorious" was, at the time, thought to be a good omen for the new state. But the city of Ostia was not truly revealed until 1938–42.

The Via Severiana (above) crosses the necropolis of the Isola Sacra, near Ostia. It was more than thirty feet wide, and divided into one section for vehicles and another for pedestrians, riders, and funeral processions.

This mosaic (left) was discovered in the Baths of Neptune at Ostia.

It must be said, however, that Mussolini's man Guido Galza made serious mistakes on the project. Rushing to meet the deadline of the 1942 Universal Exposition, he cleared only the level dating from the 2nd century AD. The more recent layers disappeared without being assessed, and the oldest layers remained buried.

Yet the exploration of Ostia was an important landmark in the history of Roman architecture, revealing for the first time the famous wheat storerooms, called *horrea,* and the *insulae,* the ancestors of modern apartment buildings. In addition, the excavation of a necropolis and the *mithrea,* small chapels where the god Mithra was worshiped, shed new light on the religious life of the 2nd and 3rd centuries AD and on the popularity of the Oriental cults that were the rivals of Christianity.

The emblem of Rome is the sacred animal of the god Mars, the she-wolf. According to legend, the wolf saved the founders of the city, Romulus and Remus, sons of Mars and the vestal virgin Rhea Silvia.

Traces of Romulus?

Like previous periods, the 20th century has yielded and continues to yield a number of masterpieces. Might Roman soil be inexhaustible? So much still remains to be excavated that it is truly impossible to estimate its riches. We still know very little, for example, about the Campus Martius. Archaeologists have to be satisfied with hypotheses formed on the basis of texts and the Forma Urbis of the 3rd century. The Circus of Flaminius, the three temples of Jupiter, Juno, and Hercules, and the Theater of Bacchus are all still hidden. We know quite precisely that, for example, we would find the ruins of the Temple of Jupiter beneath the Church of Santa Maria-in-Campitelli. But the piling up of material over the centuries has been continuous in that district of the city, and only the Portico of Octavia reflects some of its former splendor. One would have to dig very deeply indeed.

In other sites, very early material is being unearthed. Signs of life from as early as the 8th century BC, discovered by Boni on the hills, and the archaic temple discovered under Sant'Omobono around 1930 attesting to the presence of the Etruscan kings in the

6th century BC, seem to confirm the accounts of the ancient historians. The Palatine Hill may well have yielded up one of its last secrets when, in October 1988, an archaeologist found the traces of an archaic wall on the edge of the Forum. Possibly, it is the one thought to have been built in the 8th century BC as a way of defining the sacred space of the city.

Until the 20th century the discoveries were related to the imperial period or to the end of the republic. Now it is archaic Rome, the Rome of the kings, that is gradually being revealed, as though archaeology were getting closer to the origins as we get further from them in time. The Eternal City continues to reveal its secrets.

This bronze statue, the *She-Wolf*, dating from the 5th century BC, did not originally include the twins; they were added by a sculptor in the 15th century. Its first location is unknown, but Dante saw the sculpture at the Palace of the Lateran. It was moved from there to the Capitol in 1471.

Overleaf: Discovery of a statue in the 1950s (left) and excavations near the Meta Sudans in 1813 (right).

DOCUMENTS

The City Under Threat

Throughout Roman history the theme of Rome's destruction has been at the heart of people's preoccupation with the city. The need for protective measures has always been urgent.

Foreign invaders were not the only destroyers of the city. The indifference and carelessness of Romans themselves—centuries of pillage by emperors and aristocrats and ordinary citizens—played just as major a role in its devastation. Repeated appeals were addressed by the emperors to the magistrates of Rome, urging them to protect public buildings, but the sheer number of edicts proves that they were generally not effective.

EMPERORS LEO AND MAJORIAN THE AUGUST TO EMILIAN, PREFECT OF THE CITY OF ROME

In our governance of the state, we wish to correct the fact, which we have long condemned, that people are able to change the appearance of a venerable city. For it is clearly evident that the public buildings which form the entire adornment of the city of Rome are being gradually destroyed in response to the punishable suggestion of the

R uins on the Palatine, one of the seven hills of Rome and the center of political and social life during the empire.

Detail of a plan of ancient Rome.

Offices of the City. Citing the fallacious pretext of an urgent need for freestones for the construction of a public building, the admirable structures of ancient buildings are dismantled. For the restoration of some small building, large ones are being destroyed. This provides opportunities for anyone putting up a private building, by the grace of the appointed magistrates of the city, to take the necessary materials from public sites and to transport them to some other place, when in fact they form part of the city's splendor and one should therefore preserve them out of civic conscience, even where the buildings are in need of repair.

That is why we decree by this general law that nobody shall destroy or damage the whole set of buildings, that is to say, the temples and monuments founded by our forefathers, which were built for the public's use or enjoyment; this is to be enforced so that a magistrate who decides to make such an act shall have to pay a fine of fifty pounds of gold. As for employees and bookkeepers obeying his orders and not daring to resist him on their own initiative, they expose themselves to punishment by beating, and they shall also have their hands amputated— those hands with which they profane the monuments of the ancestors, when they should be preserved.

As for the places that until now individuals have claimed for themselves—a piece of mischief that must be abolished—we forbid that anything be removed from them, since, in fact, they continue to belong to the public property, and we desire that they be repaired and have restored to them those parts that have been removed, the authorization to make a claim to them having henceforth been suspended.

If urgent and overwhelming reasons make it necessary to dismantle any section, either because of the building of another public work or in order that vital repair work be undertaken, we prescribe that the issue be submitted, with all applicable information, to the venerable Senate. If after due deliberation it should consider that such action needs to be taken, the case is to be referred to our own benevolence in order that whatever we find to be beyond repair, we may order that it, at least, be transferred and made to adorn another public building, O Emilian, very dear and very affectionate father.

For these reasons, Your Illustrious Highness, please be so kind as to publish, by displaying edicts, this very salutory constitution, in order that decisions that we have taken with forethought in the interest of the Eternal City be observed with the appropriate submission and devotion.

Signed at Ravenna,
11 July AD 458

The Disappearance of a Cultural Heritage

In the course of the Middle Ages, a very large quantity of marble was burned in special limekilns and later reused as building material. Archaeologists such as Rodolfo Lanciani discovered a number of these limekilns in the 19th century.

A limekiln was found in the Palace of Tiberius on the Palatine Hill…in 1869. It was filled to the brim with fine works of art, some calcined, some intact. Among the latter were the veiled bust of Claudius now in the Museo delle Terme; a head of Nero; three caryatids in nero antico [an ornamental black marble]; the exquisite little statuette of an ephebus in black basalt…; a head of Harpocrates, and other minor fragments.

In February 1883, in the excavations on the south side of the Atrium of Vesta, a pile of marble was found about fourteen feet long, nine feet wide, and seven feet high. It was wholly made up of statues of the *Vestales maximae,* some unbroken, others in fragments. The statues and fragments had been carefully packed together, leaving as few interstices as possible between them, and the spaces formed by the curves of the bodies were filled in with chips. There were eight nearly perfect statues, and we were agreeably surprised to find among the broken ones the lower part of the lovely seated Vesta with the footstool, which, alas, is now hardly recognizable, owing to the number of

View of an 18th-century workshop for restoring antique statues.

years it has been left exposed in the dampest corner of the atrium. There were present at this remarkable discovery, which took place at 6:30 AM on February 9, only four people besides the workmen—the Crown Prince of Prussia, afterward the Emperor Frederick II, Dr. Henzen, one of my colleagues, and myself. I distinctly remember how the prince, then in the full vigour of health and strength, helped the workmen to raise the masses of marble and to set the statues up against the wall of the atrium. That was the golden age of Roman excavation, and we recall it as if it were a dream! These beautiful statues had been piled into a regular oblong, like a cord of wood, by some diggers of marbles, who had carefully filled the spaces between the statues as they lay side by side, in order that no empty spaces might be left. By what fortunate accident these sculptures were preserved it is difficult to guess; but one thing at least is certain—a great quantity of other marbles belonging to the House of the Vestals must have perished by fire. Two kilns and two deposits of lime and of charcoal were found in the course of the same excavations.

Rodolfo Lanciani
The Destruction of Ancient Rome
1901

Poggio Bracciolini's Contemplation of Rome

The contemplation of ruins inspired more than one vocation. Surveying the misfortunes of the city in 1430, Poggio Bracciolini (1380–1459) came to understand his passionate interest in Greco-Roman antiquity. Edward Gibbon (1737–94) included a description of this moment in his masterwork on the fall of the Roman Empire.

In the last days of Pope Eugenius the Fourth, two of his servants, the learned Poggius and a friend, ascended the Capitoline hill, reposed themselves among the ruins of columns and temples, and viewed from that commanding spot the wide and various prospect of desolation. The place and the object gave ample scope for moralising on the vicissitudes of fortune, which spares neither man nor the proudest of his works, which buries empires and cities in a common grave; and it was agreed that, in proportion to her former greatness, the fall of Rome was the more awful and deplorable. "Her primeval state, such as she might appear in a remote age when Evander entertained the stranger of Troy, has

been delineated by the fancy of Virgil. This Tarpeian rock was then a savage and solitary thicket: In the time of the poet it was crowned with the golden roofs of a temple; the temple is overthrown, the gold has been pillaged, the wheel of fortune has accomplished her revolution, and the sacred ground is again disfigured with thorns and brambles. The hill of the Capitol, on which we sit, was formerly the head of the Roman Empire, the citadel of the earth, the terror of kings; illustrated by the footsteps of so many triumphs, enriched with the spoils and tributes of so many nations. This spectacle of the world, how it is fallen! how changed! how defaced! The path of victory is obliterated by vines, and the benches of the senators are concealed by a dunghill. Cast your eyes on the Palatine hill, and seek among the shapeless and enormous fragments the marble

Historian Gian Francesco Poggio Bracciolini, sometimes known as Poggius.

theatre, the obelisks, the colossal statues, the porticoes of Nero's palace: Survey the other hills of the city, the vacant space is interrupted only by ruins and gardens. The forum of the Roman people, where they assembled to enact their laws and elect their magistrates, is now enclosed for the cultivation of pot-herbs, or thrown open for the reception of swine and buffaloes. The public and private edifices, that were founded for eternity, lie prostrate, naked, and broken, like the limbs of a mighty giant; and the ruin is the more visible, from the stupendous relics that have survived the injuries of time and fortune."

These relics are minutely described by Poggius, one of the first who raised his eyes from the monuments of legendary to those of classic superstition. 1. Besides a bridge, an arch, a sepulchre, and the pyramid of Cestius, he could discern, of the age of the republic, a double row of vaults in the salt-office of the Capitol, which were inscribed with the name and munificence of Catulus. 2. Eleven temples were visible in some degree, from the perfect form of the Pantheon to the three arches and a marble column of the temple of Peace, which Vespasian erected after the civil wars and the Jewish triumph. 3. Of the number, which he rashly defines, of seven *thermae,* or public baths, none were sufficiently entire to represent the use and distribution of the several paths; but those of Diocletian and

"The wonder of the Colosseum."

The Septizonium was built at the beginning of the 3rd century AD by Emperor Septimius Severus. Large parts of this building were still standing in the 16th century, when Pope Sixtus V had it completely demolished.

Antoninus Caracalla still retained the titles of the founders, and astonished the curious spectator, who, in observing their solidity and extent, the variety of marbles, the size and multitude of the columns, compared the labour and expense with the use and importance. Of the baths of Constantine, of Alexander, of Domitian, or rather of Titus, some vestige might yet be found. 4. The triumphal arches of Titus, Severus, and Constantine, were entire, both the structure and the inscriptions: A falling fragment was honoured with the name of Trajan; and two arches, then extant, in the Flaminian way, have been ascribed to the base memory of Faustina and Gallienus. 5. After the wonder of the [Colosseum], Poggius might have overlooked a small amphitheatre of brick, most probably for the use of the praetorian camp: The theatres of Marcellus and Pompey were occupied in a great measure by public and private buildings; and in the Circus, Agonalis and Maximus, little more than the situation and the form could be investigated. 6. The columns of Trajan and Antonine were still erect, but the Egyptian obelisks were broken or buried. A people of gods and heroes, the workmanship of art, was reduced to one equestrian figure of gilt brass and to five marble statues, of which the most conspicuous were the two horses of Phidias and Praxiteles. 7. The two mausoleums or sepulchres of Augustus and Hadrian could not totally be lost; but the former was only visible as a mound of earth, and the latter, the castle of St. Angelo, had acquired the name and appearance of a modern fortress. With the addition of some separate and nameless columns, such were the remains of the ancient city; for the marks of a more recent structure might be detected in the walls, which formed a circumference of ten miles, including three hundred and seventy-five turrets, and opened into the country by thirteen gates.

Edward Gibbon,
*The Decline and Fall
of the Roman Empire*, 1776–88

The Defense of the Appian Way

Ranuccio Bianchi Bandinelli (1900–75) always defended the integrity of Rome's artistic heritage. This great archaeologist, a specialist in Etruscan art, art history, and theory, who was the director general of antiquities and fine arts in Rome from 1945 to 1947, spearheaded a movement that arose at the end of World War II calling for the protection of the ruins. He proposed, for example, that great archaeological parks be created along the Appian Way.

There are few places, not only in Italy, but in the whole world, that had as much evocative and suggestive power as the Appian Way in Rome, outside the Gate of St. Sebastian. In its monuments, we read some remarkable pages of ancient history, from the end of the Roman Republic to the end of the empire, to the beginnings of Christianity and to the legends that go with it (the catacombs and the "Quo Vadis" chapel are on this road). The view we have of the walls and of the Gate of St. Sebastian is still the same as that which, for two thousand years, those born in the Mezzogiorno had of the city of Rome, the center of the Western world. After that time all of this would be destroyed and submerged beneath a flood of houses, disappearing quite simply because of a frenzy of speculation.

There are laws that protect the artistic and historic heritage, as well as the landscape. But laws are inert and impotent if there is a lack of real will to ensure that they are respected. In this case, as in a hundred others, the fault cannot be attributed to bureaucratic inertia: It lies much higher up, at the level of the government officials and, at a much higher level, in the ruling class.

It is surely symptomatic that when the alarm was sounded concerning the destruction of the Appian Way, not a single organ of the mighty middle-class press chose to champion the cause. In a hundred similar cases nobody chose to react. The whole of our incomparable artistic and cultural heritage is threatened with destruction: In the villas of the Veneto, rooms covered with Tiepolo's frescoes are being turned into stables; the Italian cities that are celebrated throughout the world as masterpieces of beauty and as the witnesses of first-rate popular culture are rapidly being transformed into something hybrid, vulgar, noisy, and colonial, like some cities in the interior of South America. (Already tourists flocking to visit the monuments are obliged to flee as soon as they can these cities that do so little to welcome them.) The ruins and remains of our old Etruscan cities, which, in terms of scholarship, are irreplaceable, are disappearing beneath the wheels of the tractors of the Ente Maremma, sacrificed to a demagogic and purely fraudulent agrarian "reform."

One could fill an entire volume with the evidence of the attacks that are successfully being mounted against the Italian artistic heritage. It would be pointless to counterbalance it with another volume of "rescue projects" carried out by the department of the arts and by other institutes whose mission it is to safeguard the cultural heritage: We know perfectly well that these organizations are doing what they can, sometimes in quite heroic working conditions. Every

The roadbed of the Appian Way.

superintendent could tell numerous stories about the pressure exerted on him by the authorities, especially by the church, to allow the laws safeguarding the cultural heritage to be overlooked and about the way in which his attempts at resistance meet with less and less support from the central authorities.

The fact is that the safeguarding of the artistic and historical heritage is one of those banners that the middle classes held high when they were rising but which they have now allowed to fall. It is one of those banners that the vanguard of the working class, the rising ruling class, now has to pick up and hold up high. It alone can fight

effectively today, including for that banner; and it will certainly find at its side many of the best representatives of the middle class, who are suffering because of what is happening but do not have the courage or the strength to fight it.

The laws and the institutes created in the past have become obsolete in the face of the attacks of the most rapacious speculators who are mounting the assault, encouraged and supported by those occupying the highest positions. The only law they know is that of lucre, of money; clerical demagogy and hypocrisy play their part. What else can one expect from the ruling class, which does not want to lead any more but merely to fill its own pockets?

A director general of the fine arts, who insisted that the distribution of a few administrators who are the directors of the departments for the protection of our cultural heritage be economically rationalized, tried to demonstrate that a few years later there would hardly be anyone left in Italy to whom one could entrust the country's artistic heritage. The best people, he said, were abandoning a difficult career, crammed with responsibilities, badly paid, and deprived of the moral support of the ruling classes.

A minister of national education in one of the De Gasperi governments replied cynically that no minister would ever take the problem seriously since there were so few of them that "they do not represent an electoral force"! Clearly, for this minister, the artistic heritage could quietly be reduced to ruins. Even on this occasion, the man appeared as a typical representative of the leading groups of his party by virtue of his lack of culture and his lack of any living link with Italian reality, a link that makes us really love our country.

However, I would not wish to mislead my readers into believing that I am being motivated here by some fetishistic cult of what is old, antique, and covered in dust. That is not the case at all; the demands of contemporary life and, above all, the need the popular Italian masses have to see their living conditions improve, make necessary, especially in the larger cities, transformations that have to be accommodated; yet it is not really those transformations that are changing the face of the Appian Way, for if the inhabitants of the shacks are certainly being evicted, they will obviously not go and live in the private villas that are being built along it. Cities have to change in appearance since they are living organisms; wanting to stop this transformation would be like wanting to stop the growth of a human being and to prevent him from changing from the beautiful child that he was into a plain old man, something we can all experience. What counts is the fostering of a consciousness of the need to build new things while intelligently respecting the old; for every old house that one destroys is an open door on history that is closed forever. Before deciding to close it, one must reflect. What counts is removing the criterion of speculation, which is the only one respected today and which has already destroyed some of the cities in our country that are most famous for their beauty.

The beauty of Italian cities is not the result of a charming piece of luck but almost always of a precise will, of directives followed by generations of city governments, the direct expression of the people. Perhaps the most typical example of this will and continuity can be found in the documents of the medieval city of Siena, in which one finds, from the mid-13th to the mid-14th centuries, a whole series of statutes and decrees setting out the building standards for the improvement of the city and giving details of facilities offered to those who contribute to such improvements; the city of Siena is today one of the most precious urban monuments of the past, an object of admiration and study for the whole world. In Verona, in the statutes of 1276, it says that no authority or office may start building without the consent of the people's council and the agreement of the "Offices of Ornamentation." The Italian people are still aware of this cultural heritage, but this awareness has to be defined, made widely known, and supported if it is to become active.

The problem is not an easy one; indeed, it is often extremely difficult. That is why we must examine it very carefully. During the Fascist period, the frenzy of real-estate speculation was disguised beneath a quite inconsistent rhetoric, which led to the disruption of the urban fabric of Rome and of other cities in the name of the "renewal of imperial goals" and to the demolition of old parts of the city because of a hatred of the "picturesque, which we do not like," or in homage to what remained of Marinetti's Futurism—one of the rare cultural experiences that was also extremely provincial, of the then leader of the country. There were occasions when the organizations safeguarding the cultural heritage were desperately trying to save a historic building and were attempting to gain some time, and the building was demolished during the night by armed gangs led by some potbellied Fascist official who was full of juvenile daring. Then, as today, the typical response of the Fascist mentality to these difficult questions is a confrontation of power. But today, there isn't even any appeal to rhetoric; today, the agents of real-estate speculation, who invest money at a profit of at least twenty-five percent, are very clever in finding the most bizarre devices in order to evade financial and technical controls. Certain of their impunity and of the complicity of those in power, who help them to evade the obligations set down by the laws regulating urban development and the limits that may be imposed by the laws protecting the artistic heritage and the landscape, they launch an open attack. One of the great scars inflicted upon the Appian Way was the building of the Pia Casa Santa Rosa, for which it was permitted that all the rules be broken "out of deference for the charitable institution." It was probably out of deference for that distinguished character that the mayor of Rome was authorized to build a house on a plot of land that the regulatory plan had destined to become a public garden.

No will, other than that of the most advanced and responsible sector of the people, can end this destruction and stop these people from doing what they are so eager to do.

Ranuccio Bianchi Bandinelli
Rome: The Center of Power, 1970

Remains of tombs along the Appian Way.

Piranesi, the Archaeologist

The appearance of Roman Antiquities *by Giovanni Battista Piranesi in 1756 made this poetic printmaker a pioneer of Roman archaeology. His conceptions of antiquity were remarkably popular in his lifetime and are still appealing today. The exceptional success of this work is explained by Piranesi's profound knowledge of engineering and architecture, combined with an outstandingly powerful imagination.*

Piranesi's engraving of the mausoleum of Caecilia Metella.

EDIFIZIO DELL'ANFITEATRO FLA-

"While stands the Coliseum, Rome shall stand; When falls the Coliseum, Rome shall fall, and when R

lls—the World." Lord Byron, *Childe Harold,* 1818

This frontispiece of the second volume of Piranesi's *Roman Antiquities* reflects his enormous interest in

...nerary architecture, especially in the tombs of the Appian Way, imaginatively reconstructed here.

The Journey to Rome

Rome has always fascinated foreigners: For centuries pilgrims, humanists, artists, and government officials have rushed to its gates, eager to admire its legendary wonders. Whether they were delighted or disappointed, their encounter with the city often inspired them to write down their impressions, which remain irreplaceable documents on the state of Rome in their time.

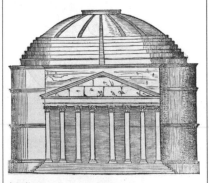

The Pantheon was built between AD 119 and 128. It is the best-preserved ancient monument in Rome today.

In AD 357 Emperor Constantius II made a pilgrimage to Rome. A historian of the time, Ammianus Marcellinus, recounts that visit.

As he went on, having entered Rome, that home of sovereignty and of all virtues, when he arrived at the rostra, he gazed with amazed awe on the Forum, the most renowned monument of ancient power; and, being bewildered with the number of wonders on every side to which he turned his eyes, having addressed the nobles in the senate-house, and harangued the populace from the tribune, he retired, with the goodwill of all, into his palace, where he enjoyed the luxury he had wished for.

And often, when celebrating the equestrian games, was he delighted with the talkativeness of the common people, who were neither proud, nor, on the other hand, inclined to become rebellious from too much liberty, while he himself also reverently observed a proper moderation. For he did not, as was usually done in other cities, allow the length of the gladiatorial contests to depend on his caprice; but left it to be decided by various occurrences. Then, traversing the summits of the seven hills, and the different quarters of the city, whether placed on the slopes of the hills or on the level ground, and visiting, too, the suburban divisions, he was so delighted that whatever he saw first he thought the most excellent of all. Admiring the temple of the Tarpeian Jupiter, which is as much superior to other temples as divine things are superior to those of men; and the baths of the size of provinces; and the vast mass of the amphitheater, so solidly erected of Tibertine stone, to the

Trajan's Forum was the commercial heart of imperial Rome.

top of which human vision can scarcely reach; and the Pantheon with its vast extent, its imposing height, and the solid magnificence of its arches, and the lofty niches rising one above another like stairs, adorned with the images of former emperors; and the temple of the city, and the forum of peace, and the theater of Pompey, and the odeum, and the racecourse, and the other ornaments of the Eternal City.

But when he came to the Forum of Trajan, the most exquisite structure, in my opinion, under the canopy of heaven, and admired even by the deities themselves, he stood transfixed with wonder, casting his mind over the gigantic proportions of the place, beyond the power of mortal to describe, and beyond the reasonable desire of mortals to rival. Therefore giving up all hopes of attempting anything of this

kind, he contented himself with saying that he should wish to imitate, and could imitate, the horse of Trajan, which stands by itself in the middle of the hall, bearing the emperor himself on his back.

And the royal prince Hormisda, whose departure from Persia we have already mentioned, standing by answered, with the refinement of his nature, "But first, O Emperor, command such a stable to be built for him, if you can, that the horse on which you purpose to make may have as fair a domain as this which we see." And when he was asked what he thought of Rome, he said that "he was particularly delighted with it because he had learned that men died also there."

Now after he had beheld all these various objects with awful admiration, the emperor complained of fame, as either deficient in power, or else spiteful, because, though it usually exaggerates everything, it fell very short in its praises of the things which are at Rome; and having deliberated for some time what he should do, he determined to add to the ornaments of the city by erecting an obelisk in the Circus Maximus, the origin and form of which I will describe when I come to the proper place.

Ammianus Marcellinus
The Roman History
Translated by C. D. Yonge, 1887

Michel de Montaigne.

"That Eagerness for New and Unknown Things"

Essayist Michel de Montaigne traveled to Italy around 1580.

Thursday, 26th of January, we went to see Mount Janiculum, on the other side of the Tiber, and closely examined the various objects of curiosity there. Among other things, [Montaigne] saw a large bit of old wall, which had come to light two days before. From this elevation you can contemplate, at one view, the whole extent of Rome, which you cannot do near so well from any other point. On leaving this place, he went to the Vatican, to see the statues which stand in niches in the Belvidere, [*sic*] and the fine gallery of paintings that the pope is collecting from all parts of Italy, and which is nearly finished. Somewhere or other in this excursion, he lost his purse and its contents; and he imagined that in giving alms, which he had done two or three times, and the weather being wet and disagreeable, in his hurry to replace his purse it had slipped down his breeches, instead of going into his pocket. Every day, he amused himself with going about and studying every part of Rome in detail. When he first arrived, he had hired a Frenchman for a guide, but this fellow having taken himself off one day in consequence of some pique, M. de Montaigne determined to do without any guide at all, beyond some maps and books that he had bought, and used to read overnight, putting the information he had thus acquired into practical use the next day; and in this way he soon made himself so thoroughly a master…

The Theater of Marcellus (above) was built in the 1st century to hold twenty thousand people. Below: Plan of ancient Rome reconstructed by the topographer Marco Fabio Calvo in 1527.

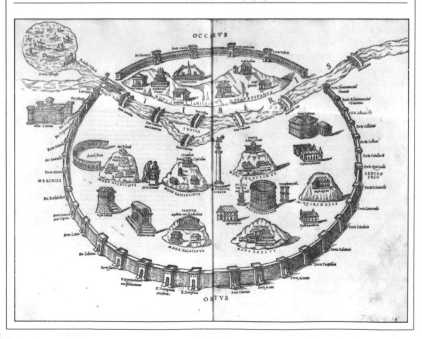

that he could have guided his guide.

He observed "that there is nothing to be seen of ancient Rome but the sky under which it rose and stood and the outline of its form; that the knowledge he had of it was altogether abstract and contemplative, no image of it remaining to satisfy the senses; that those who said that the ruins of Rome at least remained, said more than they were warranted in saying; for the ruins of so stupendous and awful a fabric would enforce more honor and reverence for its memory; nothing, he said, remained of Rome but its sepulcher. The world, in hatred of its long domination, had first destroyed and broken in pieces the various parts of this wondrous body; and then, finding that, even though prostrate and dead, its disfigured remains still filled them with fear and hate, they buried the ruin itself; that the few indications of what it had been, which still tottered above its grave, fortune had permitted to remain there, as some evidence of the infinite greatness which so many ages, so many…parricidal blows, and the never-ending conspiracy of the world against it, had not been able entirely to extinguish; but that, in all probability, even the disfigured members that did remain, were the least worthy of all those that had existed, the malignant fury of the enemies of the immortal glory having impelled them to destroy, in the first instance, that which was finest and most worthy of preservation in the imperial city; that the buildings in this bastard Rome, which the moderns were raising upon, or appending to, the glorious structures of the antique world though they sufficed enough to excite the admiration of the present age, yet

seemed to him to bear a close resemblance to nests that the rooks and the swallows construct upon the roofs and walls of the churches in France, which the Huguenots have demolished. Nay, when he considered the space which this tomb occupies, he feared that the real extent even of that was not known, he doubted whether the greater portion of the grave itself had not been

A Greek marble thought to represent Menelaus was discovered in 1501. It was the custom to write satirical comments about those in power on its base.

A 17th-century guide pointing out the wonders of ancient and modern Rome.

buried; it appeared to him that the enormous pile which, years ago, was formed merely of such miserable diggings-up, as bits of tiles and broken pots, a pile which had attained the height and size of many natural mountains (for he considered it to be as high as the hill of Gurson, and twice as large), was an express ordinance of fate, to let the world thoroughly understand, by this strange and amazing proof of grandeur, how surpassing was the glory and preeminence of the city against which they had conspired. He said he

could not at all comprehend, when he saw the limited space of some of these seven hills, especially the most famous, such as the Capitoline and the Palatine, how they could have held so great a number of buildings as have been ascribed to them. Merely looking at the remains of the Temple of Peace, the site of the Forum Romanum, the ruins of which look like a mighty mountain just fallen asunder, he could hardly understand how two such edifices could stand even on the whole space of the Capitoline hill, yet, besides these, there were on the hill twenty-five or thirty temples, besides a number of private houses. But, in truth, many of the conjectures which one has formed from pictures of the ancient city are not at all borne out when you get there, for even the site has undergone infinite changes; some of the valleys are filled up, even the deepest of them, such, for instance, as the Velabrum, which, on account of its lying so low, was selected as the main sewer of the city, and formed a watercourse, even this has now become as high as the other natural mountains which surround it, and this has solely been done by the gradual agglomeration of the ruins of old Rome; so, the Monte Savello is nothing but the heaped-up ruins of part of the theater of Marcellus. He fully believed that an ancient Roman, could one be brought back, would not be able to recognize the place. It has more than once happened that, after digging a long way down, the workmen have come to the top of some high column, which still remained standing on its base far beneath. The modern architects never think of looking for any other foundation for their houses than the tops of old buildings, the roofs of which ordinarily form the floors of modern cellars, deeming it in no way necessary to make any examination as to the foundation of the old edifice itself, or the stability of its walls; they securely base their own structure upon the ruined tops of the structure below, just as chance has happened to dispose them during the lapse of ages, and here they raise their modern palaces, as firm and safe as if the foundations were solid rocks. There are many whole streets, that stand above the old ones, full thirty feet."

Michel de Montaigne
Works of Michael de Montaigne
Vol. IV, 1887
Translated by William Hazlitt

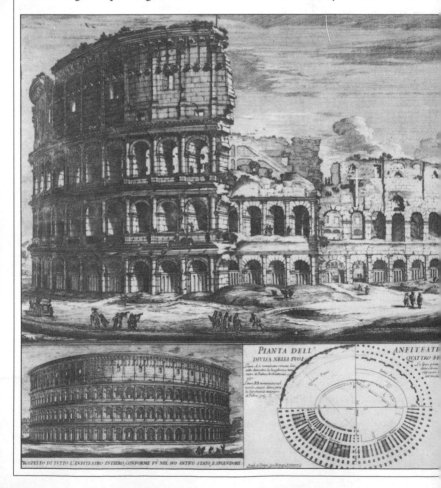

PROSPETTO DI TUTTO L'ANFITEATRO INTIERO, CONFORME FV NEL SVO ANTICO STATO, E SPLENDORE

PIANTA DELL'
DIVISA NELLI SVOI

ANFITEATI
QVATTRO PI

Propositions to Make One Shiver

In Familiar Letters Written in Italy in 1739–40, *by Charles de Brosses (1709–77), one finds a precise description of the state of the Roman*

E arly 18th-century engraving of the Colosseum.

ruins at the time and an echo of the tremendous passion they inspired.

Truly, I believe that it is difficult to find oneself for the first time amid the august solitude of the Colosseum and of the Antonine Baths without feeling a slight shiver in one's soul at the sight of the majesty of their ancient forms which were revered and abandoned. The galleries of the exterior walls of the Colosseum still provide shelter to the minor merchants who spread their wares out on poles placed in the holes from which the bronze rods in the center of the blocks of stone had been removed, as I told you. Only a semicircle of the external walls is left; it consists of four monumental floors of arcades and columns, with the bottom floor partially buried. It is held up by its own mass, in spite of the little care that is given to it and in spite of the large stones that hang from its sublime cornices; all it needs is a few repairs. There is still a full circle of lower internal galleries, but they are quite dilapidated and have a very sorry appearance. In the arena, which is quite a large oval space, one can hardly make out the ancient rows that, according to historians, could seat ninety thousand spectators. I have no trouble believing this, since the amphitheater in Verona, which is only about a third of the size of this one, can hold about thirty thousand of them. In view of the amphitheater of Verona, which has been so well repaired by its inhabitants, the Romans should be ashamed of leaving their amphitheater in such disorder, especially as it is so vast and famous and as it still has half of its finest parts; this advantage was not shared by the one in Verona, where

SPACCATO E VEDUTA INTERIORE DELL'ANFITEATRO.

Madame de Staël.

practically nothing is left of the outside wall. My plan, for I make many plans, would be to reduce the Colosseum to a semi-amphitheater, and to demolish the rest of the arches on the side of Mount Caelian, to restore the other half to its former shape and to turn the arena into a fine public square. Wouldn't it be better to have half a Colosseum in good condition than to have a whole one in tatters? And is there anything stopping you, my dear Romans, from putting a huge fountain, or even a lake, in the middle of this square, to give yourselves a reminder of your former naval power? Constantine's triumphal arch with its three gates could be one of the entrances to the square. It has been very successfully repaired in this century; the barbarians had cut all the statues' heads off; new ones have been made for them; the bas-reliefs have been mended, the pieces of marble have been put back together again; in a word, even though

this arch is a blend of good and bad taste (for in Constantine's time, the standard of work was low and the good pieces are those of Trajan's Arch, which was destroyed to be reused for this one), it is, today, one of the main antiquities of Rome, and one of the best-preserved ones.

Can you see that poor little round and low carriage-entrance near the Arch of Constantine? Fall prostrate before it, Quintus, for it is the door to what used to be Cicero's house. The place the master of the Roman Republic passed through when returning home, preceded by twelve torchbearers and followed by two thousand Roman warriors, is now only the meager atrium of some winegrower's house. What about ourselves? It is enough to scare one.

Charles de Brosses,
*Familiar Letters Written in Italy
in 1739–40,* 1799

Romantic Rome

Corinne; or, Italy, *by Madame de Staël (1766–1817), is set in Rome, where its heroes, Corinne and Oswald, discover the poetic charm of the ruins.*

Oswald could not weary of feasting his gaze from the elevated point to which Corinne had led him. The study of history can never act on us like the sight of that scene itself. The eye reigns all powerfully over the soul. He now believed in the old Romans, as if he had lived amongst them. Mental recollections are acquired by reading; those of imagination are born of more immediate impressions, such as give life to thought and seem to render us the witnesses of what we learn. Doubtless

Tourists enjoying the Campo Vaccino.

we are annoyed by the modern dwellings that intrude on these wrecks, yet a portico beside some humble roof, columns between which the little windows of a church peep out, or a tomb that serves for the abode of a rustic family, so blends the grand with the simple, and affords us so many agreeable discoveries, as to keep up continual interest. Everything is commonplace and prosaic in the generality of European towns; and Rome, more frequently than any other, presents the sad aspect of misery and degradation; but all at once some broken column or half-effaced bas-relief, or a few stones bound together by indestructible cement, will remind you that there is in man an eternal power, a divine spark, which he ought never to weary of fanning in his own breast, and reluming in those of others. The Forum, whose narrow enclosure has been the scene of so many wondrous events, is a striking proof of man's moral greatness. When in the latter days of Rome, the world was subjected to inglorious rulers, centuries passed from which history could scarce extract a single feat. This Forum, the heart of a circumscribed town, whose natives fought around it against the invaders of its territories—this Forum, by the recollections it retraces, has been the theme of genius in every age. Eternal honors to the brave and free, who thus vanquish even the hearts of posterity.

Corinne observed to Nevil that there were but few vestiges left of the republic, or of the regal day that preceded it. The aqueducts and subterranean canals are the only luxuries remaining while of aught more useful we have but a few tombs and brick temples. Not till after the fall of Sicily did the Romans adopt the use of marble; but it is enough to survey the spots on which great actions have been performed; we experience that indefinite emotion to which we may attribute the pious zeal of pilgrims. Celebrated countries of all kinds, even when despoiled of their great men and great works, exert a power over the imagination. That which would once have attracted the eye exists no more, but the charm of memory still survives.

Madame de Staël
Corinne; or, Italy
Translated by Isabel Hill, 1883

The Esthetics of Ruins

Historian Jean-Jacques Ampère (1800–64) blended travel writing and historical criticism. "Criticism has always been slightly provincial," he writes, "I wanted to let it see the world."

The poetic taste for and response to ruins did not exist in the 16th or 17th century. It emerged in France at the end of the 18th century, together with melancholy, which is hardly found in French literature before Rousseau. The century of the senses and of the mind had to arrive at it, for melancholy lies at the end of thought and pleasure. Bernardin de Saint-Pierre had already said some charming things about the grace of ruins; but the person who really revealed their poetic charm was the man who reopened for the new century the realm of religion and of the imagination, which the previous century thought it had locked up. In the *Genius of Christianity* readers had been able to admire an eloquent theory of ruins and now, here was the author of that immortal book in Rome, amid the ruins of the imperial city, which had become the great Christian metropolis. How could he fail to find there wonderful words with which to express what they inspired in him? Had he not also learned from events and from life to understand their severe language?… He was doubly prepared by his time and by his genius to feel and to express the grandiose character and the moving melancholy of the Roman ruins. He devoted only a few lines to them in a swift correspondence; but what penetrating precision one finds in the following letter:

"Whoever has no more ties in his life should come to live in Rome; there, he will find for company a land that will inspire his reflections, walks that will always tell him something. The stones he walks over will speak to him, and the dust that the wind will raise under his feet will contain some human greatness." What follows refers to Hadrian's Villa at Tivoli but describes in a marvelous way the picturesque and melancholy effects that are often reproduced in the ruins of Rome:

"Around me, through the arches of the ruins, vistas of the Roman landscape opened up: Elder bushes filled the deserted rooms where a few solitary blackbirds sought refuge; the fragments of masonry were carpeted with leaves of scolopendrium, whose green satin stood out like a mosaic upon the marble. Here and there tall cypresses took the place of columns that had fallen in these palaces of death. Wild acanthus crept at their feet over the ruins, as though nature had enjoyed reproducing on these mutilated masterpieces of architecture the decoration of their former beauty; the various rooms and the tops of the ruins looked like baskets and bunches of greenery; the wind ruffled the moist garlands, and the plants bent beneath the rain that fell from the sky."

But it was not only the ruins themselves whose physiognomy and character were perfectly expressed by the writer. That other poetry of Rome, which is more intimate and which appears only to those who consider it more carefully and with greater love, the poetry of solitary places, of deserted streets, of empty cloisters, that poetry had not been lost to him, and, beside a description of the Colosseum illuminated by the moon, it inspired him to pen the following words; I take them from a letter that is not as well known as the splendid letter to M. de Fontanes.

"Rome sleeps amid its ruins; this star of the night, a globe which one imagines to be finished and depopulated, shines down in its pale solitude on the solitude of Rome; it lights up uninhabited streets, enclosures, squares, gardens that

Antiquity incarnate greets a 19th-century traveler in Rome.

nobody crosses; monasteries in which one no longer hears the monks' voices; cloisters that are as deserted as the porticoes of the Colosseum."

Jean-Jacques Ampère
Portraits of Rome in Different Ages
1835

Travel Notebook

The novelist Emile Zola (1840–1902) journeyed to Rome in 1893.

Spent the whole day in the ruins, an indigestion of ruins, which can evoke the grandeur of Rome. In the morning, first in the Forum. The columns that remain of the Temple of Vespasian, a tremendous effect of elegance and power, against the blue sky. The Basilica Julia, only a trace, but a very clear one, on the ground. The small size of the Forum, which is always surprising when one compares it to certain monuments, the Colosseum, the Baths of Caracalla. It seems that life in Rome was sometimes restricted to very small spaces (Livia's house, etc.) and at other times spread out over considerable areas. Why? Is the problem resolved? Further on, the atrium of the Vestals, the ancient "convent" of the Vestal Virgins: interesting remains dominated by the ruins of the Palace of Caligula, which descends from the Palatine. Almost directly opposite, a church was placed within a temple of another religion. The red porphyry columns. But the main surprise is the Basilica of Constantine, with its three enormous arches, its three giant coffered vaults; the piece that fell from the vault, an enormous piece. What mass! Why were these walls so gigantic, so thick? From the Via Sacra, which passes in front

of the Basilica of Constantine, one has a very interesting view of the Forum if one turns around. The Via Sacra turns and rises. How the victors must have been shaken on their suspensionless chariots on these rough stones. The present Forum in its ruins, gray and desolate. Dust. Not a patch of grass, a few tufts of grass between the paving stones of the Via Sacra. This with the heavy sun of summer, with the narrow shadows of the few columns still standing, the Column of Phocas and those of the temples. The Arch of Septimius Severus. The rostra, etc. Temples all around. But there are ten ways of reconstructing the Forum. I am only an artist evoking the scene.

Next, I went to the Colosseum. The enormous mass, the collapsed side, the side that's standing with its bays against the blue sky. From everywhere, vaulted corridors that open out, or headless staircases, like slopes. The colossus is like a lacework of stone with all its openings against the blue sky. A blue sky above, very bright, with flights of small clouds…. A ruin baked by the sun, golden, majestic and still gigantic in its half-dilapidated state. The Arch of Titus, with its bas-relief of the defeated Jews brought back as slaves and carrying a menorah.

In the afternoon, I went to the Baths of Caracalla. It is a gigantic and inexplicable building. Two immense vestibules with areas of mosaic pavement in good condition. A frigidarium, with marks of a pool in which five hundred people could bathe at one time. Also, a vast tepidarium and a similar caldarium, with a whole system of heating furnaces still visible beside it. As well as all kinds of outbuildings whose use is unknown.

But the amazing thing is the height of the rooms, the thickness of the walls, the awesome mass of the monument. None of our medieval castles were built with this Cyclopean mass. Extravagant banks of brick and cement. It must also be said that that was all covered with precious marble and adorned with statues. An overwhelming luxury in size. For what colossal civilization? People walking around it look like ants. Today one could say crude stones, materials piled up to form Titans' homes.

Emile Zola
My Journeys: Lourdes, Rome
1955

View of the Via Sacra from the Colosseum (above). Tourists at the Forum at the end of the 19th century (below).

Parker the Photographer

John Henry Parker (1806–84), an English publisher and bookseller, visited Rome in 1863. Overwhelmed by its ancient monuments, he founded a society of archaeology lovers and organized many lectures and excursions. Around 1866 Parker began an ambitious project: to photograph the major monuments of Rome systematically. In 1879 he published the fruits of his work, a catalogue of about 3300 photographs.

Remains of the Claudian aqueduct in the Roman countryside (above and opposite). Fragments of a temple or tomb found in 1873 in the Baths of Caracalla (right).

Column topped by a sculpture (above left), and a view of the church of Santa-Croce-in-Gerusalemme (above right). Below: Traces of the Temple of Hadrian.

The Meta Sudans (above), a fountain in front of the Colosseum, was destroyed in the 1930s. The tomb of the Naso family on the Via Flaminia (below) was originally lavishly painted.

Histories of Excavations

The first archaeologists in Rome were treasure hunters. Ancient objects were sought after with the aim of making an instant profit, in terms of money or social prestige. In the first accounts of the excavations, one reads of that greed and the haste to amass objects and to amaze people.

An Artist and Antiquity

Benvenuto Cellini (1500–71) became famous as a sculptor and goldsmith. Like the other artists of his time, he drew ancient monuments and maps—and took part in the treasure hunt.

At that time, while I was still a young man of about twenty-three, there raged a plague of such extraordinary violence that many thousands died of it every day in Rome. Somewhat terrified at this calamity, I began to take certain amusements, as my mind suggested, and for a reason which I will presently relate. I had formed a habit of going on feast-days to the ancient buildings and modeling parts of them in wax or with the pencil; and since these buildings are all ruins, and the ruins house innumerable pigeons, it came into my head to use my gun against these birds. So then, avoiding all commerce with people, in my terror of the plague, I used to put a fowling-piece on my boy Pagolino's shoulder, and he and I went out alone into the ruins; and oftentimes we came home laden with a cargo of the fattest pigeons. I did not care to charge my gun with more than a single ball; and thus it was by pure skill in the art that I filled such heavy bags. I had a fowling-piece which I had made myself; inside and out it was as bright as any mirror. I also used to make a very fine sort of powder, in doing which I discovered secret processes beyond any which have yet been found; and on this point, in order to be brief, I will give but one particular, which will astonish good shots of every degree. This is, that when I charged my gun with powder weighing one-fifth of the ball, it carried two hundred paces point-blank.

It is true that the great delight I took in this exercise bid fair to withdraw me from my art and studies; yet in another way it gave me more than it deprived me of, seeing that each time I went out shooting I returned with greatly better health, because the open air was a benefit to my constitution. My natural temperament was melancholy, and while I was taking these amusements, my heart leapt up with joy, and I found that I could work better and with far greater mastery than when I spent my whole time in study and manual labor. In this way my gun…

Benvenuto Cellini.

stood me more in profit than in loss.

It was also the cause of my making acquaintance with certain hunters after curiosities, who followed in the track of those Lombard peasants who used to come to Rome to till the vineyards at the proper season. While digging the ground, they frequently turned up antique medals, agates, chrysoprases, cornelians, and cameos; also sometimes jewels, as for instance emeralds, sapphires, diamonds, and rubies. The peasants used to sell things of this sort to the traders for a mere trifle; and very often when I met them, I paid them several times as many golden crowns as they had given *giulios* for some object. Independent of the profit I made by this traffic, which was at least tenfold, it brought me also into agreeable relations with nearly all the cardinals of Rome. I will only touch upon a few of the most notable and rarest of these curiosities. There came into my hands, among many other fragments, the head of a dolphin about as big as a good-sized ballot-bean. Not only was the style of this head extremely beautiful, but nature had here far surpassed art; for the stone was an emerald of such good color, that the man who bought it from me for tens of crowns sold it again for hundreds after setting it as a finger-ring. I will mention another kind of gem; this was a magnificent topaz; and here art equaled nature; it was as large as a big hazel-nut, with the head of Minerva in a style of inconceivable beauty. I remember yet another precious stone, different from these; it was a cameo, engraved with Hercules binding Cerberus of the triple throat; such was its beauty and the skill of its workmanship, that our great Michel Agnolo [*sic*] protested he had never seen anything so wonderful. Among many bronze medals, I obtained one upon which was a head of Jupiter. It was the largest that had ever been seen; the head of the most perfect execution; and it had on the reverse side a very fine design of some little figures in the same style. I might enlarge at great length on this curiosity; but I will refrain for fear of being prolix.

The Life of Benvenuto Cellini,
Translated by John Addington
Symonds, 1888

Find After Find

Flaminio Vacca was an architect who was passionately interested in antiquities. His memoirs, the first example of an account of excavations, are a precious document about the discoveries of his time, even if his taste for anecdotes sometimes takes precedence over the truth.

I heard Gabriel Vacca, my father, say that Cardinal della Valle, who was eager to dig up treasures, had his workers dig in the Baths of Marco Agrippa, where they found a large imperial Roman gilded crown. As it resembled a kind of round cake called *gimblettes,* which were sold in the streets of Rome, the workers said: "Here is a *gimblette.*" And hoping to receive a tip, they rushed to the cardinal's home and said to him: "We have found a bronze *gimblette.*" The innkeeper who was to live in that area shortly afterward took this *gimblette* as a sign. That is why it has always been called the Gimblette.

My house, the house that I am presently living in, is built over those baths. When I wished to build a wall, I found water. By probing with a metal bar I found a Corinthian capital. It measured four spans from the base to the flower; in this it was identical to the ones in the portico of the Rotunda. There was too much water, and I had to let it rest. When building the cellar, I found a large niche entirely covered with flat terra-cotta pipes, which simply served to conduct heat in this furnace. Underneath it I found the floor, covered with slabs of marble, on which the ancients had walked; under the slabs there were thick paving stones and, under those, numerous pillars that held them up. It was between two of those pillars that the hearth had been situated; there were still ashes and coals there. We also found a large hole full of sheets of lead, fastened minutely with nails and four columns of granite that were not very tall. Then I decided to build the wall without looking further.

I remember that in the street where the Leutari live, near the Palace of the Chancellery, at the time of Pope Julius III they found a statue of Pompey beneath a cellar; it was fifteen spans high. There was a wall separating two houses over this object. The owner of one of the houses was told by the other owner that he could not have it, each of them believing that he was the owner of the statue; one of them alleged that, since he possessed the largest part of it, it should by right be his; the other said that it belonged to him because he had the head, the most important part of the statue, in his house. Finally, after all this quarreling the case went to court: The judge, an ignorant man, ordered that the head be broken off and

Section, elevation, and plan of the Temple of Peace drawn by Antoine Desgodets.

I. *Planche* DV TEMPLE DE LA PAIX, A ROME. 107

Colonne dressée deuant
S.te Marie Majeure.

Profil sur la largeur.

Profil sur la longeur

Plan de ce qui reste à present.

that each of them should get his share of the statue. Poor Pompey! It had not been enough that Ptolemy had had his head cut off, his bad luck was pursuing him even in his marble state. When Cardinal Capodiferro heard about this stupid judgment, he had it suspended and went to see Pope Julius and tell him the story. The pope was amazed; he immediately ordered that it be carefully dug up for him, and he sent five hundred crowns to the owners for them to share. Once the statue was removed he gave it to the same Cardinal Capodiferro. It was certainly a papal judgment but it took a Capodiferro [Head of Iron] to accomplish. The statue is presently in a room in his palace at the Ponte Sisto.

In my father's, Gabriel Vacca's, vineyard, beside the Porta Salaria, inside the walls, there is a piece of land that is called the Gardens of Sallust. When the ground was dug up, they found a large oval building surrounded by a portico adorned with yellow columns all around it; they were eighteen spans, tall and fluted, with Corinthian capitals and bases. This oval building had four entrances leading to marble staircases that led down to the level of the floor, made of speckled marbles laid out in beautiful patterns; at each of these entrances there stood two columns of transparent oriental alabaster. Beneath the building, we found a few pipes wide enough for a person to walk through without having to bend over all covered with slabs of Greek marble, as well as two lead pipes ten spans long and each over a span in diameter bearing the following inscription: NERONIS CLAUDIVS. Many medals of Gordian, made of silver and other metals and about the size of small coins, were also found there, as well as a large quantity of mosaics. The Cardinal of Montepulciano bought the yellow columns and used them in the building of the balustrade of his chapel in San Pietro in Montorio. He also bought the alabaster columns; he had the one that was whole polished and had the others that were broken made into tables, which he sent as a present to the King of Portugal together with other antiquities. But when they were on the high seas, impetuous Fortune, finding them in her domain, made of them a present to the sea.

On the Roman Forum, near the Arch of Septimius, I saw the extraction of great pedestals which are now in the cortile of Cardinal Farnese; they were covered with letters and names. A few

Begun in AD 206, the Baths of Caracalla (the ruins people, this complex contained a gymnasium, a

years ago, when I used to go to look at antiquities, I once found myself outside the Porta San Bastiano, at the Capo di Bove, and went into a small inn to shelter from the rain. While I was waiting and talking to the innkeeper, he told me that a few months earlier a man had come there looking for a light; he had come back that evening to have dinner with three friends, with whom he then left. But his three friends never spoke and this went on for six consecutive evenings. The innkeeper began to suspect them, fearing that they might do some evil deed, and he decided to report them. Thus, one evening, when they had just dined as usual, he followed them with the help of the moon and saw them entering some caves in the Circus of Caracalla.

The next morning he told the authorities of this and they immediately went there. Looking inside the caves, they found that a large amount of soil had been dug in which there were many pieces of pottery and vases that had only recently been broken. Scratching this soil, they found iron tools that had been used to dig that were now covered over. Wishing to shed some light on the incident and not being far from the spot myself, I went there; I saw piles of earth and the pieces of vases in the shape of jars. It is believed that these men were Goths, who had found this treasure with the help of some ancient piece of information.

Flaminio Vacca
Memoirs, 1704

...hich are shown here) were the most sumptuous in Rome. Able to accommodate sixteen hundred ...adium, an art gallery, and pleasure gardens.

Extraordinary Events

Pietro Santi Bartoli (1635–1700) was passionately interested in Roman architecture. His many attempts at pictorial reconstruction, which prefigure Piranesi's Roman Antiquities, *and his drawings of the reliefs of Trajan's Column assured him a reputation as a scholar with a sincere interest in archaeology.*

Colosseum

When digging in the garden of a certain Lady dei Nobili, to the north of the Colosseum, we found various underground rooms all nobly decorated with marble, paintings, furniture, and statues, as well as a large number of lead pipes, which enabled us to understand that this was a place of leisure that had a certain prestige.

San Gregorio

In the garden of the Cornovaglia, opposite San Gregorio, excavations have been taking place for a long time. Marvelous buildings have been seen there, underground painted rooms, porticoes, immense travertine pillars, statues, baths, busts, and a large quantity of metals; and, among other things, there was a small iron box containing all the instruments of sacrifice, and a porphyry lion that was sold to Cardinal Ghigi. But what seemed most remarkable was a room approximately twelve spans long, whose floor was covered with lead, which was raised at the level of the walls by about one span. Between this lead and the wall, where it had come slightly loose, we found a large number of gold coins; we thought that this might be the treasury of the empire or the fortune of a great personage.

Digging began again in the same place [the garden of Francesco Morelli on the Caelian hill] at the time of Clement X, and remains were found there of the most beautiful paintings to have been seen in Rome, as well as various statues and some very fine busts, especially the two *Lucius Verus* purchased by Cardinal di Buglione, as well as *Eros* and *Psyche,* bought by the Cardinal de' Medici, not to mention various other statues of speckled marble, a very fine metal lamp representing the vessel of St. Peter, and various other very fine antiquities.

Opposite this spot…they attempted to extract a treasure, but they were disappointed to find only a large number of bronze coins whose only value was that of their weight in old metal. Later, at the time of Innocent X, digging began at the level of the lower gate, leading to the alley that goes to the Colosseum, and they discovered a row of shops that seemed to have been used by coppersmiths, as there was a large number of pieces of copper there, together with the tools used to work them. Because of this and out of respect for the noble neighborhood, the excavations were ended there. They were restarted at the time of Clement X, and part of the building called Castra Peregrina was found there, in addition to some fine salt storage rooms, courtyards with their porticoes, columns made of a very beautiful breccia which were reused for the mortuary chapel of the Church of San Lorenzo-Outside-the-Walls, statues, a large number of marble heads, countless busts and metal pieces, some of which had doubtless been used for a triumphal arch, many of them being plated and encrusted with silver….

Antoniana (Baths of Caracalla)

The discovery of the Farnese Hercules was an extraordinary event: The body was found at the Antoniana, the head at the bottom of a well in the Trastevere, which was being cleared, and, last, the legs were found at Frattocchie, not far from Marino, where excavations had taken place. Today, these legs may be seen in the cellars of the Villa Borghese, among other antiquities.

The excavations that took place in the Antoniana at the time of Pope Paul III, on the orders of Cardinal Farnese, his grandson, unearthed such a profusion of statues, columns, bas-reliefs, various speckled marbles, not to mention a large number of small objects, metal statuettes, medals, oil lamps, and other similar objects, that this prince's palace became a wonderful place, as it still is today. For it alone can boast of having colossi of such an excellent style as the two *Hercules,* as well as the *Flora,* the *Gladiators,* and other statues, including that marvelous composition, the *Bull,* of stupendous size, and a large number of statues made of a single piece of marble or the countless heads, busts, and bas-reliefs that still remain heaped up, as if in storage, in two vast rooms on the ground floor. All of this, or the greatest part of it, was found at the Antoniana, apart from the bas-reliefs found in the exterior cortile where the *Bull* stands, which were found in the Piazza di Pietra, where the eleven great Corinthian columns of the portico, called the Basilica of Antoninus, can still be seen today [This monument is now identified as the Temple of Hadrian, 2nd century AD]. A portion of the marbles that were found there was discovered at the time of Innocent X, when water pipes were being connected to the fountain of the Piazza Navona; others were found during demolition of a church in order to give the place to be used by all the secondhand dealers of the Rotunda a more majestic appearance; Pope Alexander VII wanted this to be done in order to give the imposing temple a more noble character by opening up one's view of it. A few houses that were crowding in on the temple's portico were demolished, and in doing this, in the walls of that portico, they found similar statues representing Provinces [statues belonging to the Temple of Hadrian], filling the space between two columns; the best-preserved of these were then placed on the staircases of the palace of the cardinal, his grandson. Those that were found at the time of Innocent were fastened to the facade of the palace in his villa outside the Porta San Pancrazio. Others were placed on the Capitol.

Pietro Santi Bartoli,
*Memoirs of Various Excavations Made
in Rome and Surrounding Areas,*
17th century

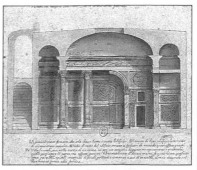

A drawing by Bartoli of a building discovered in 1683.

The French in Rome

François-René de Chateaubriand, a diplomat, sharply observed the effects of the French administration in Rome.

The first invasion of Rome by the French, under the Directorate, was infamous and accompanied by plunder; the second, under the Empire, was iniquitous: but once accomplished, order reigned.

The Republic demanded of Rome, for an armistice, twenty-two million francs, the occupation of the Citadel of Ancona, one hundred pictures and statues, and one hundred manuscripts, to be selected by the French commissaries. They especially wanted to have the busts of Brutus and Marcus Aurelius: So many people in France called themselves Brutus in those days, it was very simple that they should wish to possess the pious image of their putative father; but Marcus Aurelius— whose father was he? Attila, to go away from Rome, asked only a certain number of pounds of pepper and silk: In our day, Rome for a moment redeemed her liberty with pictures. Great artists, often neglected and unhappy, left their masterpieces to serve as a ransom for the ungrateful cities that slighted them.

The Frenchmen of the Empire had to repair the ravages the Frenchmen of the Republic had committed in Rome; they also owed a debt for the sack of Rome accomplished by an army led by a French prince: It was fitting that Bonaparte should set order in the ruins that another Bonaparte had seen grow, and whose overthrow he described. The plan adopted by the French Administration for the excavation of the Forum was that which Raphael proposed to Leo X: It caused to rise from the earth the three columns of the Temple of Concord; it exposed the pavement of the Via Sacra; it did away with the new buildings with which the Temple of Peace was encumbered; it removed the soil that covered the steps of the Colosseum, cleared the interior of the arena, and brought to view seven or eight rooms in the Baths of Titus.

Elsewhere, the Forum of Trajan was explored, the Pantheon, the Baths of Diocletian, and the Temple of Patrician Modesty repaired. Funds were put aside for the maintenance, outside Rome, of the Walls of Falerii and the Tomb of Caecilia Metella.

Repair work was also undertaken for modern edifices: St. Paul's Without the Walls, which no longer exists, had its roofing repaired; St. Agnes' and San Marino ai Monti were protected against the weather. A portion of the roof and the pavement of St. Peter's was mended; lightning rods shielded the dome of Michael Angelo from the lightning. The sites were marked out of two cemeteries in the east and west of the city, and that on the east, near the Convent of San Lorenzo, was finished.

The Quirinal arrayed its external poverty in the luxury of porphyry and Roman marbles: Designed as it was for the imperial palace, Bonaparte, before taking up his residence there, wanted to remove all traces of the abduction of the pontiff held captive at Fontainebleau. It was proposed to pull down the part of the city lying between the Capitol and Monte Cavallo, so that the triumphant might ride up to his Caesarian abode through an immense avenue; events caused these gigantic dreams to fade away by destroying enormous realities.

Among the plans decided was that of building a series of quays from Ripetta to Ripa Grande: The foundations of those quays would have been laid; the four blocks of houses between the Castle of Sant' Angelo and the Piazza Rusticucci were partly bought up and would have been demolished. A wide thoroughfare would thus have been seen from the foot of the Castle of Sant' Angelo.

The French make walks wherever they go: At Cairo, I have seen a great square, which they had planted with palm trees and surrounded with cafés bearing names borrowed from the cafés of Paris; in Rome, my fellow-countrymen created the Pincio; you reach it by a flight of stairs....

The western portion of the Piazza del Popolo was to have been planted in the space occupied by work-yards and shops; from the end of the open place

Picturesque view of archaeologists at work in the Forum, c. 1820.

Sarcophagi, urns, and funerary stelae discovered in 1775 near a vineyard.

one would have seen the Capitol, the Vatican and St. Peter's beyond the quays of the Tiber: in other words, ancient and modern Rome.

The Memoirs of François-René Vicomte de Chateaubriand, Translated by Alexander Teixeira de Mattos, 1902

A German in Rome

The author of the long History of Medieval Rome, *Ferdinand Gregorovius (1821–91) moved to Rome on the eve of Italian unification.*

18 June 1871

Rome has become a whitewashed sepulcher. The houses, and even the ancient and revered palaces, are coated with white; the rust of centuries is scraped away, and we now see, for the first time, how architecturally ugly Rome really is. Rosa has shaved even the Colosseum—that is to say, has cleared away all the plants that made it so beautiful. The Flora of the Colosseum, on which Deakin, an Englishman, wrote a book some years ago, has thus been destroyed. This transformation of the sacred city into a secular, is the reverse of the time when, with a like enthusiasm, pagan Rome transformed herself into a spiritual city. The convents are being turned into offices; the barred windows are opened, or new doors broken in the walls. After long centuries, sun and air again penetrate into these cells of monks and nuns. Thus within a short space of time St. Silvestro, the convent of the Philippines, the Minerva, the Augustinian in the [Campus Martius], the Apostolic Saints, have undergone a violent transformation. The monks who dwelt there are hounded out like badgers; it is a piteous sight to behold them stealing about ghostlike through their rooms, cloisters, and corridors. Some must rejoice at the prospect of being so soon released from their ban. Ancient Rome is fading. In the course of twenty years the world here will be a new one.

12 January 1873

Building is proceeding at a furious pace; the Monti quarter is turned entirely upside-down. Yesterday saw the fall of the lofty walls of the Villa Negroni; streets are being laid out even there; a new quarter of the city is already rising on the Praetorian Camp, another on the slopes of the Coelian beside the Quattro Coronati. Building is also going on beside St. Lorenzo in Paneperna. Almost every hour witnesses the fall of some portion of ancient Rome. New Rome belongs to the new generation, while I belong to the ancient city, in whose spellbound silence my history arose. Were I to come to Rome now for the first time, I neither should nor could conceive the idea of such a work....

2 April 1874

The convents are now almost all suppressed and deserted. Went one evening to St. Onofrio, the very eve of the day on which the monks were to evacuate the building. On entering the cloisters, saw some of them sitting silent and sad round the stone fountain; storm-clouds hung over the Janiculum, throwing the convent into shadow; the lightning flashed, and there were peals of thunder.

A Roman National Museum has been erected in St. Lorenzo in Lucina. The fate of other convents remains as

Excavating the Forum at the end of the 19th century.

yet undecided. The State archives are to be removed to the house of the Greek Basilians of S. Maria in the [Campus Martius]. The Armenians on the height beside [St. Peter's] in Vincoli keep a school, and have, consequently, been allowed to retain their quarters. But a Polytechnic Institution has fixed its abode in the monastery of [St. Peter's] itself.

In the Augustinian Monastery and at the Minerva the monks have remained on as librarians. Have not yet visited either of these libraries where for years I felt myself so much at home, and where I was always greeted with the same friendliness. Now that my name is on the Index, I do not wish to see the astonished faces of the good old men; am pained to think that many people must form unjust ideas about me, ideas that I am unable to remove.

The excavations in the Colosseum proceed apace; huge subterranean canals are brought to light. Nothing important in the way of statues has been discovered. In order to make these excavations, all the chapels of the Stations and also the Cross in the middle have been removed. This proceeding aroused a storm on the part of all the pious and in the Vatican. The Cardinal Vicar laid the Director Rosa under the ban; processions daily wound their way to the Colosseum to pray. Digging was industriously carried on.

Ferdinand Gregorovius,
The Roman Journals,
Translated by Mrs. Gustavus
Hamilton, 1911

Christian Archaeology

The discovery of the catacombs shed a great deal of new light on the funerary rites of the Early Christians. With the increasingly active assistance of the pontifical authorities, underground Rome was gradually revealed. Between 1939 and 1949 Pius XII had a search made for the tomb of St. Peter beneath the basilica. The excavations revealed an ancient necropolis and the outline of a Roman road.

A Visit to the Catacombs

If one is to believe scholar Charles de Brosses (1709–77), there was little interest in the catacombs in the 18th century. In any case, only a few of the tombs were known, and it was not really possible to visit them. The catacombs of St. Sebastian, for example, were a bandits' lair.

Charles de Brosses.

From one end to the other, I shall drop you into the catacombs; this will save you the trouble of seeing those of Rome, for these are not objects that are of interest more than once. And yet, I was foolish enough to visit those of St. Agnes, but may my example make you wise. They are long underground corridors dug into stone quarries. On each side, the stone is cut into niches, like a library.

It may be stated with certainty that

Cubicolo Primo del Cimiterio di S. Califto Papa, e d'altri Santi Martiri nelle Vie Appia, & Ardeatina.

CVBICVLVM PRIMVM
COEMETERII SANCTI CALLISTI PAPAE
ET ALIORVM SANCTORVM MARTYRVM
VIA APPIA ET ARDEATINA

Chambers in the Catacomb of St. Callistus drawn by Bosio for his book *Underground Rome.*

this was never done for any other reason than to be used as a cemetery, either since the custom of burning bodies had been abandoned, or perhaps even before that custom was introduced; at least, one might think that of the catacombs of Rome. One or more bodies were laid in each niche, after which it seems to have been sealed up in order to prevent infection. It is ridiculous and foolish to claim that they were dug by the first Christians in order to live in them and to celebrate the sacred mysteries, protected from persecution.

What fine lodgings such tunnels would make, deprived as they are of air and of light! It would be a truly fine project to have accomplished *incognito*

this whole series of wide and high corridors, a labyrinth of tunnels covering at least nine miles.

There were not enough Christians in Naples to undertake, even publicly, a project such as their catacombs, which are finer and less deep than those of Rome. I would agree that, occasionally, by chance, somebody might have hidden in them; but they were certainly never a home for the living. The remains of altars and of paintings daubed on the walls, which can be seen in quite a large room at the entrance to the catacombs of Naples, are apparently the marks of some pious ceremony which used to take place there in honor of the dead saints who were thought to have lived there.

That is all I am prepared to tell you on the subject; if you want to know more, read Misson and Burnet, who have a lot to say about it.

Charles de Brosses
Sensations of Italy
18th century

Cemetery of St. Callistus

Giovanni Battista de' Rossi discovered the catacomb of St. Callistus in 1849 and was the founder of Christian archaeology. His book Underground Christian Rome *was not only a scholarly study but an exciting account of his adventures in the depths of the earth.*

Crypt of St. Cornelius

In 1849 in the Molinari vineyard, which today is the property of the holy Apostolic palaces, I discovered a fragment of a marble plaque engraved with fine letters, on which part of the name of St. Cornelius was still inscribed:…RNELIVS MARTYR. This fragment seemed to me to belong to the epitaph that had once been placed over the sepulcher of St. Cornelius. I showed it to Father Marchi, who acquired it for the Kircherianum Museum.

Four years later, on a day in March 1852,…I walked with Father Marchi to the end of the northern path, which was partly blocked with soil, so that we had to bend down as we walked under the vault.

At the end we found a hole that had recently been dug in the tufa. Putting our heads into the hole, we saw a room full, not of soil piled up by gravediggers, but of rubble thrown in from above; faced with this, the modern plunderers, following their custom, had retreated without digging

a broader hole. My readers already know how favorable that sign is. Contemporary research is different from older methods in that we look for precisely those places that lie buried under the rubble thrown down from the openings, the stairs, or ruins of buildings that transformed the original tomb, whereas the plunderers, when they stumbled upon such places, retreated and followed the direction of the excavation made in the tufa and in soil deposits by the gravediggers of ancient times.

The event corresponded to this favorable clue.

First to appear was an arch built of good bricks, a sure sign of transfor-

Fragments of Christian inscriptions found in the catacombs (above). Ceremony in a catacomb in the 19th century (opposite).

mations and restorations of the early crypt. Then, beneath the arch, we discovered paintings; they were pictures of two saints in Byzantine style, the incontrovertible sign that there was a famous and historic crypt there. There was an inscription beside the first painting: SCI CORNELI PP, and beside the second one: . IPPI... N...

Readers remembering what I said about St. Cyprian, whose cult was associated with that of St. Cornelius, will immediately be able to complete and read the second name: CIPRIANI. Here, therefore, were Cornelius and Cyprian in a historic crypt in the cemetery of Callistus, a long way from that of St. Sixtus and St. Cecilia.

How can one doubt that this was the very tomb of St. Cornelius himself, about which topographers have given us so much precise information?

As for me, hardly had I seen the pictures when I was overcome with an incredible joy (it was the first time that I had found myself in the underground cemeteries in front of a pope's funerary monument), and I did not ask myself whether the tomb next to this painting was really the one that I imagined.

On the other side of the tomb itself we saw the effigies of two other saints in their priestly robes: The name of the first one was complete: SCS XYSTVS PP ROM; the second one's name had worn away. The tomb that was flanked by these pictures was open and without any trace of the stone or of the inscription that had once covered it.

A few Damascene letters appeared on

Entrance to a catacomb on the Appian Way.

a piece of marble that had remained affixed to the right angle above the opening of the tomb.

There was also a small fragment of a long inscription in front of the sarcophagus; it was monumental in its form and proportions and was almost Damascene in its calligraphy. Neither fragment contained a syllable that could suggest a proper name.

What was missing from the surviving lettering on the tomb was found on a third fragment discovered right inside the tomb itself. When this fragment was put next to the one I had found in the vineyard four years earlier, it fitted exactly and thus gave the full inscription: CORNELIVS MARTYR EPiscopus…

The notable and inestimable title put back together in this way, with two pieces that were discovered at different times, together with a third piece that formed the upper edge of the marble plaque, on which there were no letters, when placed on top of the tomb, covered it exactly.

The thickness of the plaque confirms and proves conclusively that it was this plaque that once formed the lid of this sepulcher; in the left corner of the tomb, one can still see, in the chalk, the mark of this precise thickness of marble.

Giovanni Battista de' Rossi
Underground Christian Rome
1864–77

Conclusion Concerning Christian Archaeology

In spite of its youth, Christian archaeology already has quite an impressive history. Philippe Pergola, a scholar working at the French National Center for Scholarly and Scientific Research and a professor of topography, describes the evolution that has occurred in the methods and objectives of this science, "which studies the archives of Early Christianity."

Has Christian archaeology changed much in the 20th century?

Christian archaeology is, today, no longer the same as that of Antonio Bosio or of Giovanni Battista de' Rossi, but it is its heir and it is proud of this parentage.

The world of Christian archaeology, like that of archaeology as a whole, brings together scholars with differing approaches: art historians, epigraphers, specialists in literary sources, and excavators with "traditional" methods (including techniques that are criticized today) or the most recent techniques (for example, the "open area" excavation perfected by British researchers).

Traditionally, Christian archaeology has concerned itself with Christian monuments from late antiquity and the early Middle Ages, especially churches, baptisteries, monasteries, and cemeteries; but, today, its field of investigation has been extended to society as a whole, including the economy and politics.

One thus speaks increasingly of late antiquity and the early Middle Ages rather than Christian archaeology. In earlier times this discipline took into consideration the monumental evidence from up to the start of the 7th century AD (the end of Gregory the Great's pontificate); today, we go right up to at least the 9th century, if not later.

All the countries of the Western

world that became Christian at the end of antiquity and at the beginning of the Middle Ages do certainly have their specialists in Christian archaeology today, but with a very few exceptions, all their activity has a link with Rome and its traditional institutions: notably, the Pontifical Commission for Christian Archaeology, which has, since the mid-19th century, supervised the excavation and administration of the Roman catacombs, and the Pontifical Institute of Christian Archaeology, which was founded in 1925 and accepts students from all over the world who go there for three years to prepare doctoral dissertations in their particular fields.

What are the great discoveries and the great debates of the last thirty years in this field?

It is almost impossible to list them. Many monuments have been excavated, and their discovery has often cast doubts on firmly entrenched beliefs. To focus on Rome only and the domain of the catacombs, several theories have been overturned, thanks especially to the renewal of scholarly study and problematics.

In Rome the most spectacular discovery was that of a catacomb on the Via Latina that was richly decorated with particularly unusual paintings. Besides biblical images, which were totally unknown in this form or were very unusual when compared to the hundreds of other cycles known until now in the Roman catacombs, the owners of this private complex had also had entirely pagan scenes painted.

This complex, which may be dated roughly between AD 330 and 380, contrary to all speculation on the part of the archaeologists and historians of late antiquity, is the proof of a definite tolerance and of a close union, up to and beyond death, between Christians and pagans.

As for the catacombs themselves, recent studies have made it possible to establish that they were not originally specifically Christian but that, in fact, independent of all religious affiliation, they were resorted to systematically, in the early decades, and that this type of burial inside underground tunnels was universal.

Finally, in the last thirty years, Christian archaeology has swelled its ranks and its field of action with the help of stratigraphic excavations carried out by the researchers of the most recent generation; these "fine" excavations have often made it possible to revise the chronology of a number of monuments, but they have also given us a different image of the end of antiquity and of the early Middle Ages: There was no break prompted by the invasions of bloodthirsty barbarians, but instead we witness a long transition toward the Middle Ages, with progressive changes in every domain. The Lombards, for example, were rehabilitated thirty years ago; the Vandals are also now being rehabilitated: Their arrival in Africa did not break any of the traditional economic circuits, and the destruction caused by their passing or by their settling in certain provinces now appears only in the writings of those nostalgic for outdated theories that are unequivocally contradicted by all the archaeological discoveries of the last few years.

Further Reading

Andreae, Bernard, *The Art of Rome,* Harry N. Abrams, New York, 1977

Bianchi-Bandinelli, Ranuccio, *Rome: The Center of Power,* George Braziller, New York, 1970

———, *Rome: The Late Empire,* Thames and Hudson, London, 1971

Boëthius, Axel, *The Golden House of Nero,* University of Michigan Press, Ann Arbor, 1960

Gibbon, Edward, *The Decline and Fall of the Roman Empire,* Random House, New York, 1932

Grabar, André, *Early Christian Art,* Odyssey Press, New York, 1968

Gregorovius, Ferdinand, *The Roman Journals,* trans. Mrs. Gustavus W. Hamilton, George Bell & Sons, London, 1911

Krautheimer, Richard, *Early Christian and Byzantine Architecture,* Penguin Books, Baltimore, 1975

Lanciani, Rodolfo, *The Destruction of Ancient Rome,* Benjamin Blom, New York, 1967

L'Orange, H. P., *Art Forms and Civic Life in the Late Roman Empire,* Princeton University Press, Princeton, New Jersey, 1965

MacKendrick, Paul, *The Mute Stones Speak: The Story of Archaeology in*

Italy, St. Martin's Press, New York, 1960

Marcellinus, Ammianus, *The Roman History,* trans. C. D. Yonge, George Bell & Sons, London, 1887

McKay, A. G., *Houses, Villas, and Palaces in the Roman World,* Cornell University Press, Ithaca, 1975

Pollitt, J. J., *The Art of Rome c. 753 BC–AD 337, Sources and Documents,* Prentice-Hall, Englewood Cliffs, New Jersey, 1966

Potter, Timothy, *Roman Italy,* University of California Press, Berkeley, 1987

Ramage, Nancy and Andrew, *Roman Art: Romulus to Constantine,*

Harry N. Abrams, New York, 1991

Salmon, E. T., *The Making of Roman Italy,* Thames and Hudson, London, 1982

Simon, Erika, *Ara Pacis Augustae,* New York Graphic Society, Greenwich, Connecticut, 1967

Toynbee, J. M. C., *Death and Burial in the Roman World,* Thames and Hudson, London, 1971

Ward-Perkins, John B., *Roman Architecture,* Harry N. Abrams, New York, 1977

Wheeler, R. E. M., *Roman Art and Architecture,* Thames and Hudson, London, 1964

List of Illustrations

Key: a=above; b=below; c=center; l=left; r=right

Abbreviations:
BN=Bibliothèque Nationale, Paris; ENSBA=Ecole Normale Supérieure des Beaux-Arts, Paris

Front cover Jacques Carlu. View of the citadel on the Capitol, detail. Gouache and watercolor on paper, 1924. ENSBA
Spine Victor Jean Nicolle. *Trajan's Forum.* Watercolor, c. 1800. Cabinet des Dessins, the

Louvre, Paris
Back cover Sebastiano Ricci. *Architectural Caprice with Roman Ruins.* Painting. Private collection, Switzerland
1 Louis Duc. The Colosseum in its restored state. India ink and wash drawing, 1830. ENSBA
2–3 Louis Duc. The Colosseum in its restored state (detail). *Ibid.*
4–5 Jacques Carlu. View of the citadel on the Capitol. Gouache and watercolor on paper, 1924. ENSBA
6–7 Constant Moyaux.

Restored state, plan of the Tabularium and the monuments located at the foot of the Capitol. India ink and watercolor, 1866. ENSBA
8–9a Ferdinand Dutert. Restored elevation of the Forum based upon the excavations and texts. India ink and watercolor, 1874. ENSBA
8–9b Ferdinand Dutert. Present state of the Forum. India ink and watercolor, 1874. ENSBA
11 Bridgens. Excavations in the Forum. Colored engraving, c. 1820.

Museum of Rome
12 Map of Rome in Fazio degli Uberti, *Dittamondo,* 14th century. BN
13 Figure of Rome with the globe. Diptych, AD 496. Museum of Roman Civilization, Rome
14 Constantine leading Pope Sylvester to the Gate of Rome and offering him the crown. 12th-century fresco in the Oratory of St. Sylvester, Rome
14–5 Engraving (detail), 19th century

16al The Circus Maximus. Colored engraving, 17th century. Collection Nardecchia, Rome

16bl The Pyramid of Caius Cestius. Colored engraving, 16th century

16r Cross section of Trajan's Column. Engraving, 16th century

17l Trajan's Column. Engraving

17ar Roberto Schezen. View of the dome of the Pantheon

17br Etienne Du Pérac. The Pantheon. Drawing, 16th century. Collection Nardecchia, Rome

18–9 Maerten van Heemskerck. The Colosseum. Drawing, 1532–6. Cabinet des Dessins, the Louvre, Paris

20–1 Rome in the 8th century. Chromolithograph in the *Einsiedeln Itinerary*, 8th–9th century

21 Nicolas Poussin. Equestrian statue of Marcus Aurelius. Drawing, 17th century. Musée Condé, Chantilly, France

22 Title page of a *Mirabilia*. Wood engraving, 1550

22–3 Colossal bronze head of the emperor Constantine, early 4th century. Capitoline Museum, Rome

23 Emperor Frederick II. Engraving

24–5 Andrea del Castagno. *Petrarch*. Painting, early 15th century. Sant'Apollonia, Florence

25 Portrait of Cola di Rienzo. Engraving

26 Bronze tablet, 1st century AD. Capitoline Museum, Rome

27 Plan of Rome in the form of a lion.

Manuscript, late 13th century. MS 151, Staats- und Universitäts- bibliothek, Hamburg

28 Georges Chédanne. *Nero's Domus Aurea, the Hall of the Laocoön*. Painting. Musée des Beaux-Arts, Rouen, France

29 The Limbourg brothers. Plan of Rome in *Les Très Riches Heures du Duc de Berry*, 15th century. Musée Condé, Chantilly, France

30–1 Miniatures of Rome from Giovanni Maricanova, *Codex Mutinesis*, 1465. Biblioteca Estense, Modena, Italy

32a Anonymous. Room in the Vatican library in the 17th century

32–3b The Temple of Venus and Rome. Copy after Palladio. Drawings Department, Kunstbibliothek, Staatliche Museen Preussischer Kulturbesitz, Berlin

33a Miniature in a 14th-century edition of Livy's *History of Rome*

34a Anonymous. Portrait of Julius Pomponius Laetus. Engraving

34b Portrait of Pope Paul II. Engraving

34–5 Paul Bril. *View of Rome with the Castel Sant' Angelo*. Painting, 1600. Tower of the Winds, the Vatican

35b Facsimile bronze tablet containing text of Claudius' speech in support of Gaul's request to be represented in the Roman senate, c. AD 48. Museum of Roman Civilization, Rome

36l Raphael. Decoration of a Vatican loggia. Painting, early 16th century. Vatican City

36r Grotesque on a vault of a Vatican loggia. Vatican City

37 Reproduction of grotesque ornaments in the Domus Aurea. In Pietro Santi Bartoli, *Drawings of Ancient Paintings*, 17th century

38b Raphael. *Portrait of Pope Julius II*. Painting, early 16th century. Vatican City

38–9a Federico Zuccari. Taddeo Zuccari drawing *The Laocoön Group*. Drawing, mid-16th century. Uffizi Gallery, Florence

39b *The Laocoön Group*. 1st century AD. Vatican Museums

40l Raphael. *Portrait of Leo X*. Painting, 1518. Uffizi Gallery, Florence

40–1 The *Apollo Belvedere*. 4th century BC. Pio-Clementino Museum, Vatican City

41 Maerten van Heemskerck. *Cortile di Casa Sassi à Roma*. Drawing, c. 1535. Drawings Department, Kunstbibliothek, Staatliche Museen Preussischer Kulturbesitz, Berlin

42–3 Tomb of Augustus. Engraving in Alo Giovannoli, *Views of Ancient Roman Ruins*, 1619

43 Fragment of the Forma Urbis. Marble, AD 205–8. Museum of Roman Civilization, Rome

44a Pirro Ligorio. Plan of Hadrian's Villa. Drawing, c. 1550

44b Charles Natoire. Hadrian's Villa. Watercolor, 1772. Musée Atger, Montpellier, France

45a Bayot. Ruins of Hadrian's Villa. Lithograph

45b Mosaic of doves from Hadrian's Villa. Capitoline Museum, Rome

46–7 Pirro Ligorio. Plan of Rome with what may still be seen of the ancient monuments. Colored engraving, 1551

48al Giorgio Vasari. The building of St. Peter's. Fresco, mid-16th century. Palace of the Chancellery, Rome

48ar Anonymous. *Portrait of Pope Sixtus V*. Engraving. Palace of Versailles, France

48–9 Maerten van Heemskerck. The state of St. Peter's Basilica between 1520 and 1536. Drawing, c. 1536. Uffizi Gallery, Florence

49a Frontispiece of Domenico Fontana, *Della Trasportatione dell'Obelisco Vaticano*, 1590

50–1 Giovanni Guerra. Setting up the obelisk in St. Peter's Square. Colored engraving, 1586. Collection Nardecchia, Rome

52a Portrait of Charles V. Painting, 16th century. Musée Condé, Chantilly, France

52–3 Anonymous. *The Sack of Rome*. Painting. Private collection, Paris

53a Maerten van Heemskerck. The death of Charles, duke of Bourbon, during the sack of Rome in 1527. Engraving, 1555

54a Engraving from Antonio Bosio, *Underground Rome*, 1632

54b *Idem*

55a *Idem*

55b *Idem*

56–7 Paul Bril. *The Forum*. Painting, c. 1600. Rijksmuseum, Amsterdam

58 Michael Sweerts. *The Painting Studio*. Painting,

c. 1650. Rijksmuseum, Amsterdam

59 Abraham-Louis-Rodolphe Ducros. *The Square of the Capitol with the "Dioscuri."* Watercolor, 18th century

60a Bartolomeo Cavaceppi. Self-portrait. Engraving, 18th century

60b Jacques Sablet. *A Visit to the Antiquarian.* Painting, 1788. Private collection, Rome

61 Johann Zoffany. *Charles Townley in His Gallery.* Painting, late 18th century. Towneley Hall Museum and Art Gallery, Burnley, England

62–3 Willem van Haecht. *The Studio of Cornelis van der Geest.* Painting, 17th century. House of Rubens, Antwerp, Belgium

64a Entrance to the underground ruins of Otricoli. Lithograph, 1802. Collection Nardecchia, Rome

64b Jacques Sablet. View of the gardens of the Villa Borghese in Rome. Watercolor, 18th century

65 Johann Wilhelm Baur. *Facade of the Villa Borghese.* Painting, 17th century. Borghese Gallery, Rome

66–7 Philippe Agricola. *The Founding of the Chiaramonti Museum.* Chiaramonti Museum, Vatican City

68al and **bl** Tomb of the Scipios

68–9 Francesco Bianchini. Columbarium of the Emancipated People, built by Augustus. Engraving in Giovanni Battista Piranesi, *Camere Sepolcrali degli Antichi Romani,* c. 1750

69a Giovanni Battista Piranesi. Tomb of the Scipios. Engraving in Piranesi, *Roman Antiquities,* 1756

70–1 Charles Natoire. The terrace of the Farnese Gardens on the Palatine Hill. Pencil and wash drawing, 1759. Cabinet des Dessins, the Louvre, Paris

71a *The Temple of Saturn, Enclosed Within a Series of Houses, at the End of the 18th Century.* Watercolor. Collection Nardecchia, Rome

71b Stadium of Domitian on a 2nd-century coin

72–3 Abraham-Louis-Rodolphe Ducros. *View of the Palatine Hill with the Arch of Constantine.* Painting, 18th century

73a Charles Natoire. *The Palatine.* Watercolor, 18th century. Kunstbibliothek, Staatliche Museen Preussischer Kulturbesitz, Berlin

74 Giovanni Battista Piranesi. Frontispiece in Piranesi, *Il Campo Marzio dell'Antica Roma,* 1762

74–5 Giovanni Battista Piranesi. View of the Campo Vaccino. *Ibid.*

75ar Giovanni Battista Piranesi. *Self-Portrait.* Engraving

75cr Fragments of ruins

75b Giovanni Battista Piranesi. Engraving, 18th century

76–7 Canaletto. *The Colosseum and the Arch of Constantine.* Painting, 18th century. Christie's, London

78–9 Bernardo Bellotto. *View of the Forum Boarium and of the Temple of Fortuna Virile.* Painting, mid-18th century

80–1 Giovanni Pannini. *Gallery of Ancient Rome.* Painting, 1757. The Louvre, Paris

83l Angelica Kauffmann. Portrait of Johann Joachim Winckelmann.

Painting, 1764

83r Frontispiece of Johann Joachim Winckelmann, *History of Ancient Art,* 1764

84 Hubert Robert. *Excavations Inside the Colosseum.* Painting, 18th century. The Prado, Madrid

85 Louis Duc. Plan of the Colosseum. Drawing, 1830. ENSBA

86–7a Anonymous. Departure from Rome of the third convoy of statues and artistic monuments for the National Museum in Paris, on 10 June 1797. Engraving

86–7b Francesco Hayez. *The Return to Rome of the Works of Art Carried off by the French.* Painting. Chiaramonti Museum, Vatican City

87a Théophile Auguste Vauchelet. *Portrait of Ennio Quirino Visconti.* Painting, 19th century. Musée Carnavalet, Paris

88a Portrait of Quatremère de Quincy. Engraving

88b *Galley Slaves Working on the Excavations.* Lithographs in Thomas, *One Year in Rome,* 1830

89 Théophile Auguste Vauchelet. *The Roman Forum.* Painting on velvet, 19th century. Fontainebleau, France

90–1a Scaffolding to raise the mass of the architrave of the Temple of Jupiter Tonans. Drawing, 1812. Museum of Rome

90–1b Bartolomeo Pinelli. The Temple of Jupiter Tonans before (left) and after (right) the Napoleonic excavation and restoration

90–1b *Insets* Plans of the Temple of Jupiter

before (left) and after (right) the Napoleonic excavations, 1813. Archives Nationales, Paris

91ar Jacques-Louis David. *Portrait of Pope Pius VII.* Painting, c. 1800. The Louvre, Paris

92a Portrait of Count Pierre Antoine Daru. Engraving

92–3 Angelo Uggeri. Remains of the Baths of Titus. Pencil and wash drawing in *Journées Pittoresques,* 1817

93a View of the excavations of the Basilica of Constantine during the Napoleonic administration. Ink drawing. Archives Nationales, Paris

93b Camporensi. Plan of the state of the excavations of the Domus Aurea in 1811. Archives Nationales, Paris

94a Victor Jean Nicolle. View of Trajan's Forum and Column. Drawing, c. 1800. Cabinet des Dessins, the Louvre, Paris

94b *Trajan's Forum After Its Clearing.* Watercolor. Lanciani Archives, Biblioteca dell'Istituto d'Archeologia e di Storia d'Arte, Rome

95 Construction of the Vendôme Column in Paris. Painting. Château de la Malmaison, France

96a Angelo Uggeri. The Temple of Concord. Pencil and wash drawing in *Journées Pittoresques,* 1817

96b Portrait of Giuseppe Valadier. Engraving

96–7 J.-F. Ménager. Reconstruction of the Temple of Antoninus and Faustina. Drawing and detail, 1809. ENSBA

97a Abraham-Louis-Rodolphe Ducros and

Giovanni Volpato. The Temple of Antoninus and Faustina. Watercolor, c. 1775

98–9 After Bartolomeo Pinelli. Working on the Pincio in Rome. Lithograph

100 Discovery of the *Righetti Hercules*. Photograph, 1864. Museum of Rome

101 Bronze equestrian statue of Marcus Aurelius on the Capitol

102 *Augustus of Primaporta*. Chiaramonti Museum, Vatican City

103a Fresco from the House of Livia. National Museum of Rome

103c Pietro Campana. The Tomb of Pomponius Hylas. Lithograph in Campana, *De Due Sepolcri Scoverti tra la Via Latina*, 1843

104a Pierre Martin Gauthier. The Basilica of Constantine. Drawing, 1814. ENSBA

104b Giustino Carocci. Portrait of Antonio Nibby. Engraving, 19th century

105a and **b** Excavations in the Forum during the Napoleonic occupation. Ink drawings

106–7 Giovanni Battista Cipriani. Remains of the buildings of ancient Rome. Lithograph, 1815. Collection Nardecchia, Rome

108–9 Oswald Achenbach. The Tomb of Caecilia Metella. Painting, late 19th century. Christie's, London

110 Luigi Canina. Tomb on the Appian Way. Engravings in Canina, *La Via Appia*, 1850

111 Luigi Canina. Present state and reconstruction of the Casal Rotondo. *Ibid.*

112–3 The Catacombs. Engravings in Giovanni Battista De' Rossi, *Underground Christian Rome*, 1864–77

114–5 Pope Pius IX visiting the catacombs with Giovanni Battista De' Rossi. Lithograph

116 American tourists in the catacombs. Illustration, 1900

117 Discovery of a skeleton in the depths of Rome. Illustration, 1900

118 John Henry Parker. Fragments of sculptures found on the Palatine. Photograph, 1870

118–9 Engraving of the Institute of Archaeological Correspondence. Frontispiece of the German Archaeological Institute's *Unpublished Monuments*, mid-19th century

119a John Henry Parker. Entrance to the Catacombs of St. Domitilla. Photograph, 1870

120 Discovery of the *Seated Gladiator*. Photograph, 1885

121 The *Seated Gladiator*. Bronze. National Museum of Rome

122a John Henry Parker. View of the excavations of the Temple of Minerva Medica. Photograph, 1871

122b John Henry Parker. Objects found during the building of the new city. Photograph, 1874

123a Fresco from a house near the Farnesina. National Museum of Rome

123b Stucco from a villa near the Farnesina. National Museum of Rome

124 Portrait of Giacomo Boni. Lithograph

125a The interior of the Colosseum before the excavations of 1885

125b The interior of the Colosseum after the clearing of the underground passages

126–7 Nino Carnevali. *Minister Guido Baccelli Visiting the Excavations of the Forum*. Painting

127 Minister Guido Baccelli in front of the presumed Tomb of Romulus in the Forum in 1899. Lithograph

128b Portrait of John Henry Parker

128–9b Rodolfo Lanciani. Plan of the Forum. Drawing, 1910

129b John Henry Parker. Arch of Titus. Photograph, c. 1870

130–1 Mussolini wielding the pickax to open the excavation of the Via dell'Impero

131al Roman Eagle, symbol of victory. Cameo, AD 27. Kunsthistorisches Museum, Vienna

131ar Mussolini as Augustus

132a Procession of the family of Emperor Augustus. Southern frieze of the Ara Pacis

132l A figure from a frieze on the Ara Pacis

132–3b Reconstruction of the Ara Pacis

133a The Ara Pacis

134–5 Bruno Brizzi. Reconstruction of the Colosseum of Rome

136–7 Model of ancient Rome. Museum of Roman Civilization, Rome

138–9 Becchetti. Reconstruction of the northern part of the Roman Forum. Watercolor. Biblioteca della Soprintendenza alle Antichità di Roma, Rome

140a Marble masks found in the Theater of Ostia

140–1b Mosaic in the Baths of Neptune, Ostia

141a The Via Severiana, near Ostia

142–3 The *She-Wolf*. Bronze, 5th century BC (twins added in the 15th century). Capitoline Museum, Rome

144 Discovery of a statue in Rome in the 1950s

145 Bartolomeo Pinelli. Excavations around the Meta Sudans in 1813. Engraving

146 Ruins on the Palatine Hill. Engraving in Sadeler, *Ruins of Ancient Rome*, 1906

147 Pirro Ligorio. Plan of ancient Rome. Engraving, 16th century

148 Studio for the restoration of antique statues in the 18th century. Engraving

149 Portrait of Poggio Bracciolini. Engraving

150 View of the Colosseum. Engraving

151 Etienne Du Pérac. The Septizonium on the Appian Way. Engraving

153 The pavement on the Appian Way

155 The Appian Way

156–7 Giovanni Battista Piranesi. The Tomb of Caecilia Metella on the Appian Way. Engraving in Piranesi, *Roman Antiquities*, 1756

158–9 Giovanni Battista Piranesi. The Colosseum. *Ibid.*

160–1 Giovanni Battista Piranesi. Frontispiece showing Roman funerary architecture. *Ibid.*

162 Sebastiano Serlio. The Pantheon. Engraving in Serlio, *De Architectura Urbis*, 1565

163 Giovanni Antonio Dosio. Trajan's Forum. Engraving

164 Alphonse Leroy. *Portrait of Michel de Montaigne*. Engraving

165a Theater of Marcellus. Engraving in Sadeler, *Ruins of Ancient Rome*, 1906
165b Marco Fabio Calvo. Plan of ancient Rome. Drawing, 1527
166 Antoine Lafreri. "Pasquino" (Menelaus). Engraving, 16th century
167 Guide for foreigners. Engraving, 17th century
168–9 The Colosseum. Engraving, early 18th century
170 Portrait of Madame de Staël
171 Tourists in Rome in the Campo Vaccino. Lithograph
173 Bartolomeo Pinelli. The Spirit of Antiquity confronting the Roman traveler. Engraving, 1818
175a View of the Via Sacra from the Colosseum
175b The Forum and the Arch of Septimius Severus. Photograph, late 19th century

176b John Henry Parker. Remains of a temple or tomb discovered in the Baths of Caracalla. Photograph, c. 1870
176–7a John Henry Parker. The Claudian aqueduct. Photograph, c. 1870
177b John Henry Parker. Reservoir for the Claudian aqueduct. Photograph, c. 1870
178al John Henry Parker. Column topped by a sculpture. Photograph, c. 1870
178ar John Henry Parker. View of the cloister of Santa-Croce in Jerusalem. Photograph, c. 1870
178b John Henry Parker. Temple of Hadrian reused by the pontifical authorities. Photograph, c. 1870
179a John Henry Parker. The Meta Sudans, remains of a fountain in

front of the Colosseum. Photograph, c. 1870
179b John Henry Parker. Tomb of the Naso family on the Via Flaminia. Photograph, c. 1870
181 Portrait of Benvenuto Cellini. Engraving
183 Antoine Desgodets. The Temple of Peace. Engraving in Desgodets, *The Ancient Monuments*, 1682. BN
184–5 The Baths of Caracalla. Engraving in Alo Giovannoli, *Views of Ancient Roman Ruins*, 1619
187 Pietro Santi Bartoli. Cross section of a building discovered in 1683. Drawing. Print Room, BN
189a Work being done on the Forum around 1820. Drawing
189b Large sarcophagi, urns, and funerary stones of the imperial era, discovered in 1775 near a

vineyard. Engraving
191 Excavations of the Argileto Forum
192 Portrait of Charles de Brosses. Engraving
193 First chamber of the Catacombs of St. Callistus. Engraving in Antonio Bosio, *Underground Rome*, 1632
194 Fragments of Christian inscriptions found in the catacombs. Engraving in Giovanni Battista De' Rossi, *Underground Christian Rome*, 1864–77
195 Celebration of the Feast of St. Cecilia in the Catacombs of St. Callistus. Engraving, 1887
196–7 Entrance to a catacomb. Engraving in Giovanni Battista De' Rossi, *Underground Christian Rome*, 1864–77
206 Fragments of statues among ancient ruins. Engraving

Index

Page numbers in italics refer to captions and/or illustrations

A

Adrian VI, pope 40–1
Aemilia, Basilica *126*
Agonalis, Circus of 151
Agrippa 17, *132*
Alaric the Visigoth 15
Albani, Cardinal Alessandro 65, *83*; Villa of 65
Alberti, Leon Battista, *Description of Rome* 33
Alexander, popes: VI 49; VII 187
Ampère, Jean-Jacques 172–4
Annals (Tacitus) 35

Antoninus and Faustina, Temple of 96, *96–7*, *126*, 127
Apollo, Temple of 108
Apollo Belvedere 40–1, 86
Appian Way 61, *68–9*, 101, 108–10, *109–11*, 160–1, *196–7*
Ara Pacis 45, 132, *132–3*
Augusto Imperatore, Piazza 132
Augustus, emperor 20, 70, 102, 110, 130, *131*, Arch of 48; Forum of 131, 132; Tomb of 42, *42*, *108*, 151
Augustus of Primaporta 102, *102*, 128
Aula of Isis 73

B

Bandinelli, Ranuccio Bianchi 152–5
Barbatus, sarcophagus of 68, 70
Bartoli, Pietro Santi *37*, 186–7
Belvedere, Vatican 40–1, 164
Benedict, Canon 22
Biondo, Flavio: *Roma Instaurata* 36; *Roma Triumphans* 36
Boni, Giacomo 124, *124*, 126, 127, 128, 142
Borghese, Villa of *64–5*
Bosio, Antonio 54–5, *54*, 60, 112, 198
Bracciolini, Gian Francesco Poggio 30,

31, 32, 33–4, 36, 54, 149–51, *149*
Brosses, Charles de 169–70

C

Calvo, Marco Fabio *165*; *Antiquities of Rome* 52
Campana, Marquis Giovanni 102–3
Campo Vaccino 14, *75*, *171*; see also Forum
Campus Martius *74*, 82, 142
Canina, Luigi 108, 110
Canova, Antonio 87, *87*, 89
Capitoline Hill 20, 23, 40–1, *46–7*, 103
Caracalla, emperor, Baths

of 42, 151, 174, *177*,
185, 187
Carceri (Piranesi) 82
Casal Rotunda *111*
Castagno, Andrea del
24–5
Castel Sant' Angelo *31*,
34, 67, 189
Castor and Pollux,
Temple of 89
Catacombs 55, 60, 101,
112–3, *112–9*, 192–8,
193–5, *197*
Cavaceppi, Bartolomeo
60, 61, *61*
Cellini, Benvenuto *36*,
52, 180–2, *181*
Charles V, emperor 30,
52, *52*, *70*
Chiaramonti Museum,
Vatican *67*, *87*, 102
Christian archaeology 55,
60, 194, 198–9
Claudius, emperor *35*;
aqueduct of 50
Clement, popes: VII *34*;
X 186; XI 65, *77*; XIV
61, 66, *67*
Colosseum 17, *18–9*, 21,
24, *33*, 38, 49, *76–7*,
80–1, *84–5*, 95, 96,
104, 124, *125*, *134–5*,
150, 151, 169, *169*,
174, 188
Commission for the
Embellishment of
Rome 92, 98
Commission for Antique
Monuments and Civic
Buildings 92
Concord, Temple of 96,
96, 103, 188
Constantine I, emperor
14, *15*, 17, *21–3*, 41,
73; Arch of *73*, *80– 1*,
89, 151, 170; Basilica
of 96, 104, *104*, 174;
Baths of 151
Constantius II, emperor
17, 162–4
Cyriacus of Ancona 31, 54

D

Damasus I, pope 113
De Architectura
(Vitruvius) 33
De' Rossi, Giovanni
Battista 112–4, 194–8

Description of Rome
(Alberti) 33
*Description of the Superb
and Very Rich Villa
Adriana* (Ligorio) 45
de Staël, Madame 170–2
De Urbe Roma (Rucelli)
33
Dictionary of Antiquities
(Ligorio) 48
Diocletian, emperor,
Baths of 14, 50, 124,
150–1, 188
Dioscuri 59, *118*
Dittamondo (Uberti) *12–3*
Domitian, emperor 71;
Baths of 151; Palace of
71–3; Stadium of *71*,
124
Domus Aurea (Golden
House) 14, *29*, *37*,
38–40, 45
Dondi, Giovanni 26, 31
Dying Gaul 80–1

E

Einsiedeln Itinerary 20,
21–2, 60, 104
Emilian, prefect of Rome
146–8
Esquiline Hill *122*, 123

F

Farnese, Cardinal
Alessandro 71, 123;
Garden of 71, *72*;
Palazzo of 123; Villa of
123–4, *123*
Farnese Hercules 80–1
Fascism 128, 130–42,
154–5
Fea, Carlo 89, 98, 103,
104, 141
Flaminius, Circus of 142
Fontana, Domenico *48*,
49, 50
Forma Urbis 42, *43*, *74*,
82, 105, 142
Forma Urbis, The
(Lanciani) *129*, *135*
Fortuna Virile, Temple of
78–9
Forum 14, 20, 23, *33*,
46–7, 49, *70*, 89, *89*,
98, 101, 103, 104, 105,
105, 110, *118*, 124,
126, 128, *129*, *138–9*,

143, 162, 167, 174,
175, 184, 188, *189*
Francis I, king of France
40, 41
Frederick II, emperor *23*,
24–5, 148

G

Gagliardi, Giuseppe 102
Gallery of Ancient Rome
(Pannini) *80–1*
German Archaeological
Institute 118, *118*
Gregorius, Master *21*,
23–4
Gregorovius, Ferdinand
122, 190–1
Gregory, popes: XIII 49;
XVI 112
Gregory the Great 60–1,
198
Griffins, House of the 73

H

Hadrian, emperor *33–4*;
Temple of 61, *178*,
187; Tomb of 151;
Villa of *44*, 45, *45*, 61,
172–4
Hercules, Temple of
78–9, 142
History of Ancient Art
(Winckelmann) 83
Hylas, Pomponius, Tomb
of *103*

I

Innocent, popes: II 22;
VIII 41; X 186
Italian School of
Archaeology 124
Itinerary (Cyriacus of
Ancona) 31

J

Janiculum *46–7*
Julius, popes: II *38*, 40;
III 42
Jupiter, Temple of *91*,
104, 108, 142, 162
Justinian, emperor *23*

L

Laetus, Julius Pomponius
31, 34–5, *34*, 118

Lanciani, Rodolfo 20,
121, 123, 124, 128,
132, *135*, 148–9
Laocoön Group, The 28–9,
39–40, *80–1*, 86, *93*
Lateran, Basilica of the
25, *26*, 67; Palace of the
143
Leo, emperor 146–8
Leo X, pope 40, *40–1*, 188
Ligorio, Pirro *44*, 45, *45*,
47, 48, 52
Livia, House of *103*, 108

M

Majorian, emperor 146–8
Marcellinus, Ammianus
162–4
Marcellus, Theater of
151, *165*, 167
Marcus Aurelius, emperor
21, *30*, *101*; Column of
51
Mare, Via del 131
Maximus, Circus of
16–7, *73*, 151
Meta Remi *16*
Meta Sudans *143*, *144*,
179
Metella, Caecilia, Tomb
of *108*, 110, *157*, 188
Michelangelo 40, 110,
188
Minerva Medica, Temple
of *122*
Mirabilia Urbis Romae
(Marvels of Rome)
22–3, *22*
Mommsen, Theodor
108, 114
Montaigne, Michel de
14, 164–8
"Mostra Augustea della
Romanità" 132, *135*,
140
Museum of Roman
Civilization *135*
Museum of the Roman
Empire 132
Mussolini, Benito 95,
130–1, *130–1*, 140

N

Napoleon Bonaparte 40,
86, 87, 90, *95*, 99, 188
Naso family, Tomb of the
179

National Museum of Rome 124
Neptune, Baths of *141*
Nero, emperor 38, 68; Circus of 50, *50–1*
Nibby, Antonio 103–4, 105, 108
Nicholas V, pope 32

O

Ostia 50, 98, 131, 140–2, *140–1*
Otricoli *64–5*

P

Palatine Hill 17, 20, *46–7, 70,* 71, *72–3,* 108, *118,* 124, 127, 143, *146,* 148, 167, 174
Palladio, Andrea 33, *33*
Pannini, Giovanni *80–1*
Pantheon 17, *17,* 20, 21, 24, *99,* 150, *162,* 163, 188
Papyri of Monza 60–1

Parker, John Henry *118,* 128, *128–9,* 176, *177–9*
Parma 71, 72
Patriarchum, Lateran 50
Patrician Modesty, Temple of 188
Paul, popes: II *34;* III 49, *70,* 123
Peace, Temple of *93,* 104, 150, 167, 182, *183,* 188
Pergola, Philippe 198–9
Petrarch 25, *25*
Philip II, king of Spain 41
Philip IV, king of France 24
Pinciana, Villa 66
Pio-Clementino Museum, Vatican 66–8, *66–7,* 70
Piranesi, Giovanni Battista *68–9, 74,* 75, *75,* 82, *156–61*
Pius, Antoninus *96*
Pius, popes: IV 48; V 40–1; VI 66–8, 70, 85, 86; VII *67,* 88, 89,

91, 95, *95;* IX 102, 114, *114,* 141
Pliny the Elder 40
Pompeii 74, *83,* 90
Pompey, Theater of 17, *101,* 151, 163
Popolo, Piazza del *99,* 189
Poussin, Nicolas *21,* 75

Q

Quincy, Quatremère de 87–8, *88*
Quirinal Hill 123, 127, 188

R

Raphael *36, 38,* 39, *40–1,* 51, 52, 86, 110, 188
Rienzo, Cola di 25–6, *25, 26*
Righetti, Cardinal, Palace of *100–1*
Roman Academy 34–5, 118

Roman Antiquities (Piranesi) 82, *156–61*
Romulus, Temple of 104
Rucelli, Bernardo 33, 36

S

Sacra, Via 174, *175,* 188
St. Peter's Basilica 21, 22, *31, 48,* 49, *49,* 50; Square of *51*
St. Philip Neri, Oratory of 54
St. Sylvester, Oratory of *14–5*
Santa Croce, Oratory of 50–1
Saturn, Temple of *71, 89,* 103
Schliemann, Heinrich 112
Scipios, Tomb of the 68, *68,* 70
Seated Gladiator 120–1
Septimius Severus, emperor 50, *71;* Arch of 89, *89, 127,* 151,

174, 184; Septizonium
of 50
Severiana, Via *141*
She-Wolf 41, *143*
Sixtus, popes: IV 35, 41,
48, *77;* V 50, 123, *151*
Spinario (*A Boy Picking a
Thorn from His Foot)*
41, *80–1*, 86
Sylvester, pope *14–5*

T

Tabularium *91*, 103
Tacitus, *Annals* 35
Theodoric I, king of the
Visigoths 17
Tiberius, emperor, Palace
of 148

Titus, emperor, Arch of
80–1, 96, *129*, 151,
174; Baths of *93*,
151, 188
Trajan, emperor, Baths of
14, 38, *93;* Column of
16–7, 21, 51, 93, *94–5*,
98, 151; Forum of 17,
93, 95, *96*, 163, *163*,
188

U

Uberti, Fazio degli,
Dittamondo 12–3
Ulpia, Basilica of 95
*Underground Christian
Rome* (De' Rossi) *112*,
114

Underground Rome
(Bosio) *54–5*, 55
Universal Exposition of
Rome *135*, 142

V

Vacca, Flaminio *42*,
182–5
Vasari, Giorgio *48*, *63*
Vatican 86, 164; Belve-
dere 40–1, 164; Library
32, *32*, 48; Palace 39;
Pio-Clementino
Museum 66–8
Venus and Rome, Temple
of *33*, 96, 103
Vespasian, emperor 25,
26, 104, 150; Temple

of *56–7*, *80–1*, 91,
104, 174
Victor Emmanuel II, king
of Italy 124
Views of Rome (Piranesi)
82
Vitruvius, *De Architectura*
33

W

Winckelmann, Johann
Joachim *29*, 59, 82–3,
82–3

Z

Zola, Emile 174–5
Zuccari, Federico *39*

Acknowledgments

The author wishes to thank Filippo Coarelli and Alain Borer for reading the manuscript; Noëlle de la Blanchardière for her advice and encouragement; and Claude Nicolet and Charles Pietri for their kind assistance. Thanks also go to those individuals and organizations who helped with the realization of this work: Annie Coarelli, bookseller in Rome; Philippe Morel, art historian at the Villa Medici; Fausto Zevi, director of the Institute of Art History and Archaeology of Rome; Pierre Pinon, architect; and Nicole Thirion, translator, Editions Robert Laffont

Photograph Credits

Text Credits

Claude Moatti, Ph.D., specializes in the study of political
thought and the crisis in culture that arose at the end of
the Roman Republic and in the early Roman Empire
(2nd century BC to 1st century AD). At the same time
Dr. Moatti is now doing research on the history of the
discovery of ancient Rome and the "invention" of
Roman archaeology. In this book she presents
the first findings of her project.

For Thomas

Translated from the French by Anthony Zielonka

Project Manager: Sharon AvRutick
Editor: Linda Epstein
Typographic Designer: Elissa Ichiyasu
Cover Designer: Robert McKee
Editorial Assistant: Jennifer Stockman
Design Assistant: Penelope Hardy
Text Permissions: Neil Ryder Hoos

Library of Congress Catalog Card Number: 92–82805

ISBN 0–8109–2839–6

Printed and bound in Italy by Editoriale Libraria, Trieste